Master the Art of Building Your Ultimate Gaming PC

Zarahx E. Thomas

Funny helpful tips:

Engage with books that promote environmental awareness; they offer insights into our relationship with nature and sustainability.

Maintain a strong online presence; digital visibility is crucial in today's market.

Master the Art of Building Your Ultimate Gaming PC : Unleash Your Gaming Potential with Expert Techniques for Crafting Your Perfect PC Setup

Life advices:

In the forest of challenges, stand tall, drawing strength from your roots and vision.

Cultivate a strong personal brand; it's how you present yourself to the world and can open opportunities.

Introduction

Welcome to this book, your comprehensive manual to create the ultimate gaming rig tailored to your needs and preferences. In this guide, we'll walk you through each component of a gaming PC and provide valuable insights to help you make informed decisions.

First, we'll provide an overview of the key computer components, including the all-important Graphics Card and Central Processing Unit (CPU). Understanding these components is crucial to building a high-performance gaming system.

The Graphics Card is the heart of any gaming PC, and we'll delve into the differences between AMD and Nvidia options, as well as explore various graphics card manufacturers, VRAM, and FPS capabilities.

Next up is the Processor (CPU), where we'll explain the differences between Intel and AMD processors, clock speeds, cores, threads, cache memory, and more. You'll gain clarity on choosing the right CPU for your gaming needs.

Ensuring your gaming PC runs smoothly requires the right cooling system. We'll guide you through choosing an appropriate CPU Cooler to keep your processor performing at its best.

System Memory (RAM) plays a crucial role in gaming performance, and we'll discuss how much RAM is needed, memory speed, latency, and help you make the right memory choice.

Storage is vital for gaming, and we'll explore different Hard Drive options, including space, speed, and types, to ensure your games load quickly and efficiently.

To complete your gaming PC build, we'll explain the importance of choosing the right Motherboard, considering factors like ports, chipsets, and compatibility with other components.

Every gamer needs a reliable Computer Case to house their components. We'll discuss case sizes, cooling options, and help you pick the ideal case for your setup.

Powering your gaming PC is crucial, and our guide to the Power Supply Unit (PSU) will explain wattage, efficiency, modular vs. non-modular, and other critical factors to consider.

With your gaming PC ready, we'll help you choose the perfect Monitor for immersive gaming experiences, covering aspects like aspect ratio, resolution, response times, and more.

Finally, we'll guide you through the process of building your gaming PC, including the BIOS setup and installing Windows 10. You'll have all the information you need to finish your gaming masterpiece.

Get ready to embark on an exciting journey of building your gaming dream machine with confidence and expertise. Let's power up your gaming experience to new heights!

Contents

Computer Components Overview

Graphics Card

A graphics card is also known as a video card. The graphics card's job is to send graphics to the monitor. Shown below.

CPU (Central Processing Unit)

The CPU (aka processor) is the brains of the computer. It's the computer's main microchip that will process computer data and instruct the other components on what to do next. Shown below.

CPU Cooler

The CPU cooler (usually consisting of a fan) will keep the CPU from overheating. Shown below.

System Memory (RAM)

The computer's system memory (aka memory or RAM) is used to store the data of opened files and programs so that they can be accessed quickly by the CPU. Shown below.

Optical Drive

An optical drive can be a DVD drive, Blu-ray drive or a CD drive that can read various disks (DVD movies, DVD games, music CD's and so on). Some of the optical drives can also write to a disk. Shown below.

Hard Drive

The hard drive is used to store all of the computer's data such as photos, videos, games, music and so on. Windows itself is also stored on the hard drive. Shown below.

Motherboard

The motherboard (aka mainboard) is the main circuit board that connects all of the other computer components together. Shown below.

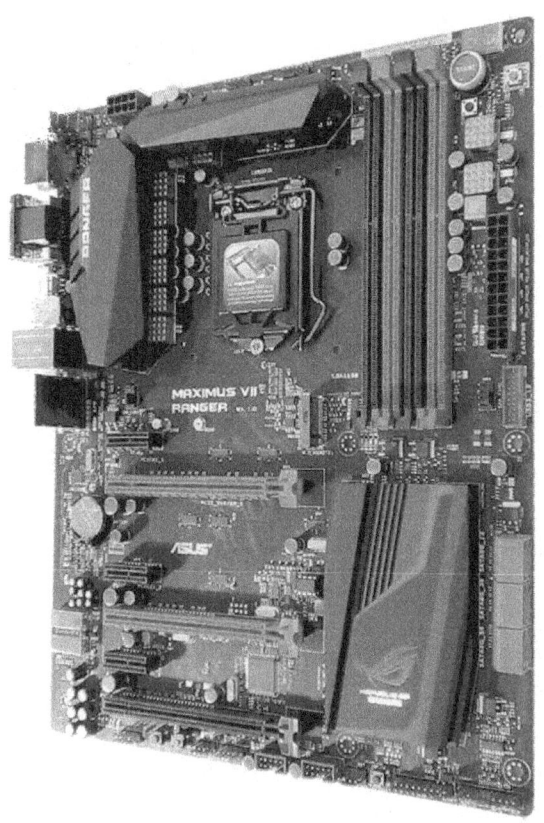

Computer Case

The computer case is used to house all of the computer's internal components. Shown below.

PSU (Power Supply Unit)

The PSU (aka power supply) is used to power all of the internal components inside the computer case. Shown below.

Computer Build Example

Here's how a computer looks inside when finished. Shown below.

The Graphics Card

There's no doubt that the graphics card is the most important part of a computer when it comes to building a gaming PC. If you have a great graphics card, your games will look amazing. Well, at least the games that are designed with great graphics will look amazing.

The other computer components have a role to play in all of this too, but the graphics card takes centre stage when it comes to bringing games to life on a PC. So let's go through what they're all about, so that you can get yourself a graphics card that's right for you. You'll then have the best gaming experience your budget will allow.

AMD vs Nvidia

There are two main graphics card companies... AMD (formally ATI, taken over by AMD) and Nvidia.

So which graphics card is the best to use for gaming, AMD or Nvidia? Well some games are designed with AMD in mind so those games should perform better with an AMD graphics card. Some games are designed with Nvidia in mind so those games should perform better with an Nvidia graphics card. But often this doesn't make much difference and sometimes makes no difference at all.

So what about price? The performance of AMD and Nvidia graphics cards are often very similar at every price point. This will vary a little from time to time but generally speaking both AMD and Nvidia put out similar performing graphics cards for a similar price. So neither of them come out on top when it comes to price.

Sometimes AMD will produce the most powerful graphics card that money can buy, but Nvidia will then counter strike and bring out one that's even better. The company that have the best graphics card at any one time will tend to change every so often.

So the answer is to just go for the graphics card that suits you as it doesn't really make much difference whether you choose AMD or Nvidia. Having said all that, many gamers choose Nvidia as they often use less power, but both AMD and Nvidia make some great graphics cards.

Nvidia Graphics Cards

Nvidia's latest generation of graphics cards are referred to as the '900' series. Here are their latest offerings in order of performance, starting with their most powerful card.

NVIDIA GeForce Graphics Cards (900 Series)

Model Name - Performance
GTX Titan X - High end
GTX 980 Ti - High end
GTX 980 - High end
GTX 970 - Upper Mid Range
GTX 960 - Mid Range
GTX 950 Lower Mid-Range

Before the '900' series was the '700' series from Nvidia. Here they all are, again in order of performance, starting with the most powerful graphics card.

NVIDIA GeForce Graphics Cards (700 Series)

Model Name - Performance
Titan Z - High End
Titan Black - High End
Titan - High End
GTX 780 Ti - High End
GTX 780 - High End
GTX 770 - Upper Mid Range
GTX 760 - Mid Range
GTX 750 Ti - Lower Mid Range
GTX 750 - Lower Mid Range
GT 740 - Low End
GT 730 - Low End

GT 720 - Low End

All the graphics cards listed were the latest offerings from Nvidia at the time of writing. For an up to date list of Nvidia graphics cards, go to:

http://www.geforce.com/hardware/desktop-gpus

There were other graphics cards before the '700' series, but they're too out dated now to be included in the list. Not only that, trying to get yourself an older one (from say the '600' series) would be quite difficult as few companies even stock them any more. Graphics cards from the '700' to the '900' series will give you a very wide range of choice, so you're not missing out on anything here.

Nvidia Graphics Card Model Names Explained

You'll see graphics cards advertised as, for example, *'Nvidia GeForce GTX 960'*. So let's talk about the numbers in the Nvidia model names above. Nvidia graphics cards with a *10, 20, 30 or 40* at the end of its model name (for example, the GTX 740) is a low-end graphics card. A Nvidia graphics card with a *'50'* in its model name (e.g. GTX 750) is a lower mid-range graphics card. A *'60'* in the name is a mid-range card, *'70'* in the name will be upper mid-range and *'80'* or above are all high-end graphics cards.

Then there's the *'Titans'* which are very high-end cards, often with a high-end price tag to go with it.

Also there are *'Ti'* versions of certain graphics cards. The *'Ti'* basically means that it's a faster version of the same card. So for example the '*Nvidia GeForce GTX 780 Ti* ' and the '*Nvidia GeForce GTX 780'* are very similar in how they perform, but the *Nvidia GeForce GTX 780 Ti* graphics cards have an extra boost in performance.

When comparing similar graphics cards from one series to another, the latest series will be the best for performance and graphics. So for example, the GTX 960 from the 900 series will be more powerful than the GTX 760 from the 700 series.

By the way, all the graphics cards in the lists just mentioned come under the 'GeForce' umbrella. Let me explain briefly. Nvidia make graphics cards for home/gaming computers. Those are all called 'Nvidia GeForce'. But Nvidia also make other graphics cards such as Nvidia Tesla and Nvidia Quadro. Tesla cards are for big number crunchers (scientists and the like), and Quadro cards are for workstations. For a gaming PC though, you'll want a 'Nvidia GeForce' graphics card, if you're going with Nvidia.

AMD Graphics Cards

The latest generation of graphics cards from AMD are called the 'Rx 300' series. Here are their newest cards in order of performance, starting with their most powerful graphics card.

AMD Radeon R9 300 Series Graphics Cards (enthusiast range)

Model Name
R9 Fury X
R9 Fury
R9 390 X
R9 390
R9 380

AMD Radeon R7 300 Series Graphics Cards (mainstream range)
Model Name
R7 370
R7 360

Before the 300 series of AMD graphics cards were the 200 series. Here they are in order of performance, most powerful first.

AMD Radeon R9 200 Series Graphics Cards (enthusiast range)
Model Name
R9 295X2
R9 290X
R9 290
R9 280X
R9 285

R9 280
R9 270X
R9 270
AMD Radeon R7 200 Series Graphics Cards (mainstream range)
<u>Model Name</u>
R7 265
R7 260X
R7 260
R7 250X
R7 250
R7 240
AMD Radeon R5 200 Series Graphics Cards (non-gamers range)
<u>Model Name</u>
R5 230

All of the graphics cards listed were the latest offerings from AMD at the time of writing. For an up to date list of AMD graphics cards, go to:

http://www.amd.com/en-us/products/graphics/desktop

AMD Graphics Card Model Names Explained

Generally speaking, the higher the number in the graphics card's model name, the better the graphics card will be. For example, the *'AMD Radeon R9 285'* is more powerful than the *'AMD Radeon R9 280'*.

Within the AMD 300 series, all of the *'R9'* graphics cards are more powerful than all of the *'R7'* graphics cards. And within the AMD 200 series, all of the R9 graphics cards are more powerful than the R7's. Then we have the least powerful which is the R5 in the AMD 200 series.

Remember that when comparing similar graphics cards from one series to another, the latest series will be the best for performance and graphics. For example, the *AMD Radeon R9 390X* is more powerful than the *AMD Radeon R9 290X*.

Graphics Card Manufacturers

We've been discussing AMD and Nvidia graphics cards, but when you browse the various cards on offer, they will be advertised as, *for example*, 'Asus Nvidia GeForce GTX 780' or 'Gigabyte Nvidia GeForce GTX 980' or 'Sapphire AMD Radeon R9 280X' and so on. This is because AMD and Nvidia only make the main microchip for the graphics card. These microchips called GPUs (Graphics Processing Units) are sent to other companies. These companies then make the rest of the graphics card and solder the GPU onto it. So when you see, *for example*, an 'Asus Nvidia GeForce GTX 980' graphics card, the *'GTX 980'* part is the main microchip (GPU) and Asus make the rest of the graphics card (circuit board, cooling fans etc.).

Graphics Card Memory (VRAM)

Every graphics card will have its own memory built onto the card itself. This memory is called VRAM (Video Random Access Memory). So you may see graphics cards advertised as, for example, *'MSI Nvidia GeForce GTX 970 4GB'*. The VRAM will hold graphical information about the game that's being played, ready to be sent to the monitor.

Many graphics cards these days have 2GB – 4GB of VRAM. Some of the very high-end cards have 6GB or above. The more VRAM you have the better, but more VRAM on a graphics card will make it a little more expensive to buy. As a guide, for those playing graphically intense games, the following amount of VRAM would be very good for today's games.

Monitor Resolution VRAM
1920 x 1080 2GB – 3GB
2560 x 1440 3GB – 4GB
3840 x 2160 4GB – 6GB

Note that the recommendations here are just a guide for graphically intense games. Many games that are not so graphically intense may require less VRAM than is stated above. Again, this is just a guide.

FPS (Frames Per Second)

Camcorders these days often record at 30 FPS. In other words they take 30 pictures per second to make up a smooth looking video when played back. Imagine if they only took 5 pictures per second. The video would look very stuttery and not smooth at all. Well, it's a similar story when playing video games. The better your graphics card is, the more FPS it can produce and the smoother your games will look.

Here's a few examples of how many FPS two different graphics cards can produce at various monitor resolutions. All three games shown are graphically intense. *Results will vary from one PC to the next.*

Game-- Monitor Resolution--Graphics Card--FPS (average)

BioShock Infinite--1920 x 1080--Nvidia GTX 770--**120**
Tomb Raider (2013)--1920 x 1080--Nvidia GTX 770--**60**
Crysis 3--1920 x 1080--Nvidia GTX 770--**55**

BioShock Infinite--2560 x 1440--Nvidia GTX 770--**50**
Tomb Raider (2013)--2560 x 1440--Nvidia GTX 770--**45**
Crysis 3--2560 x 1440--Nvidia GTX 770--**40**

BioShock Infinite--3840 x 2160--Nvidia GTX 770--**30**
Tomb Raider (2013)--3840 x 2160--Nvidia GTX 770--**25**
Crysis 3--3840 x 2160--Nvidia GTX 770--**20**

BioShock Infinite--1920 x 1080--Nvidia GTX 750 Ti--**55**
Tomb Raider (2013)--1920 x 1080--Nvidia GTX 750 Ti--**45**
Crysis 3--1920 x 1080--Nvidia GTX 750 Ti--**35**

As you can see from the list shown, the lower your monitor's resolution is, the more FPS the graphics card can produce. Also, the less graphically demanding the game is, the more FPS the graphics card can produce. The Nvidia GTX 770 graphics card is more powerful (and more expensive) than the Nvidia GTX 750 Ti, so it's no surprise that the Nvidia GTX 770 can produce more FPS.

Some gamers are happy with 30 FPS for fairly smooth game play. Many gamers prefer 40 FPS for smooth game-play. Some gamers prefer 50 - 60 FPS for extremely smooth game play.

So basically it comes down to this... the more you spend on a graphics card, the more FPS it will be able to produce, therefore the smoother your game-play will look.

Something to note here... a monitor labelled as 60Hz can show 60 FPS. 60Hz is the minimum for all monitors, so *all* monitors can display at least 60 FPS. A monitor labelled as 120Hz can show 120 FPS. A monitor labelled as 144Hz can show 144 FPS... I think you get the idea. Anyway, if you're using a 60Hz monitor, you'll see up to 60 FPS from the graphics card, even if your graphics card can produce over 60 FPS.

So let's say you have a graphics card that can push out 70 FPS on a particular game and you're using a 60Hz monitor. In this case you'll be seeing 60 FPS. If your graphics card is pushing out, let's say, 35 FPS and you're using a 60Hz monitor, you'll see 35 FPS. 120Hz monitors can show up to 120 FPS from the graphics card and 144Hz monitors can show up to 144 FPS from the graphics card.

Graphics Card Ports

Every graphics card will have at least one port at the back of the card itself. Every monitor will also have at least one port. Those two ports can be connected up via a cable so that the graphics card can send information directly to the monitor for display.

Here are the ports you may see on the back of a graphics card and monitor. Shown below.

 **HDMI Port** 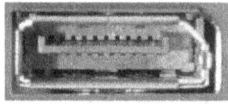 **DP DisplayPort**

 **VGA Port**  **DVI Port**

So if you have, for example, a monitor with a HDMI port, then you'll also want to have a graphics card with a HDMI port so that the two ports can be connected up via a HDMI cable. You can buy converter cables for when you don't have a match. For example, let's say you have a monitor with a DP port and a graphics card with a HDMI port. In this case, you could get a DP to HDMI converter cable to link the two ports up, but it's best to get a match in the first place.

All of the ports just shown (and the cables they use) can support at least 1920 x 1200 monitor resolution at 60Hz. So whichever type of ports/cables you use, they will support at least 1920 x 1200 monitor resolution running at 60 FPS. I know many gamers use full HD monitors (1920 x 1080 resolution) at 60Hz, so this will be good news for many. So let's go through each type of port, one by one, to see what they're all about.

HDMI (High Definition Multimedia Interface)

Many graphics cards and monitors today have HDMI version 1.4 ports. HDMI 1.4 is capable of supporting up to a 4k (3840 x 2160) monitor resolution at 24Hz - 30Hz. So if your graphics card and monitor both have an HDMI 1.4 port (connected via an HDMI cable), then the best you can get when using a 4k monitor is 30 FPS. In some gamers eyes, this won't be enough FPS for their liking. But when using a monitor with 2560 x 1440 resolution or less, you'll be able to achieve at least 60 FPS using HDMI 1.4.

Some of the newer graphics cards and monitors have HDMI version 2.0 ports. HDMI 2.0 is capable of supporting up to a 4k (3840 x 2160) monitor resolution at 60Hz. This means that if you use a graphics card and a 4k monitor, both of them having an HDMI 2.0

port, then you can connect the two up and enjoy a 4k monitor resolution, playing games at a maximum of 60 FPS.

All HDMI versions are all fully backwards and forwards compatible with each other. Which ever is the lower version will be its maximum capability. For example, if you have a graphics card that has an HDMI 1.4 port, coupled with a 4k monitor that has an HDMI 2.0 port, you'll be able to experience up to a 4k resolution at 30 FPS, not 60 FPS.

DP (DisplayPort)

Just like HDMI 2.0 just mentioned, *'DP version 1.2'* can support up to a 4k monitor resolution (3840 x 2160) at 60Hz (60 FPS).

Earlier versions of DP may support up to 3840 x 2160 at 30 Hz. DP is the only current connection that can support G-Sync (more on that in the 'Monitor' section of this book). And of course, if you're going use DP ports, you'll need a DP cable.

VGA (Video Graphics Array)

VGA technology can support up to 2048 x 1536 monitor resolution at 85Hz (85 FPS).

VGA is the oldest technology of the four and is quickly going out of style. Rarely do you see a graphics card with a VGA port these days. It's an analogue technology that was originally intended for CRT monitors (those big bulky monitors that weigh a ton). Computers deal with digital data, but CRT monitors are analogue So a VGA connection would convert a digital signal from the computer, to analogue for a CRT monitor to display. VGA technology has poor image quality compared to HDMI, DisplayPort and DVI.

DVI (Digital Visual Interface)

There are various types of DVI connections. Here they all are:

DVI - I Dual Link

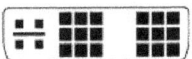

DVI - I Single Link

DVI - D Dual Link

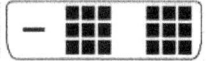

DVI - D Single Link

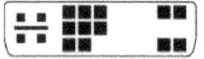

DVI - A

The only DVI connection types you'll see on graphics cards these days (if they have one) are 'DVI-I dual link' *(aka DVI-I DL)*and possibly 'DVI-D dual link' *(aka DVI-D DL)*. That's been the case for many years now.

If your monitor and graphics card both have a DVI-I dual link port, you can connect them up using a *'DVI-I dual link'* cable. If your monitor and graphics card both have a DVI-D dual link port, you can connect them up using a *'DVI-D dual link'* cable. If you don't have matching ports, you can use an adapter such as a DVI-I DL to DVI-D DL, or a DVI-I DL to HDMI adapter.

Single link DVI-I and DVI-D can support a monitor resolution of up to 1920 x 1200 at 60Hz.

Dual link DVI-I and DVI-D can support a monitor resolution of up to 2560 x 1600 at 60Hz.

Although DVI technology is still very much used today, it's starting to become less popular as DisplayPort 1.2 and HDMI 2.0 are starting to break through more and more with better support for higher resolutions, Ethernet and audio, all through a single cable. DVI and VGA technologies can only send video through their cables.

SLI and Crossfire

SLI (Scalable Link Interface) is a Nvidia thing. When you have two or more Nvidia graphics cards working together in one PC, that's called an *SLI* configuration. AMD's version of this (two or more AMD graphics cards working together in one PC) is called a *Crossfire* configuration.

If you have two identical graphics cards in a computer, the second card may give you up to 100% more graphics power. But adding a third graphics card may give you up to 2.8 times the power (according to Nvidia). So let's say that you have a Nvidia GTX 760 graphics card that can produce 25 FPS in a particular game. Adding a second Nvidia GTX 760 card may then give you 50 FPS. Adding a third Nvidia GTX 760 card may give you up to 70 FPS *(in this example)*.

Results from having two or more graphics cards can vary a lot though. For example, adding a second graphics card may give you a 100% performance boost for one game, while in another game you may see 50% extra performance.

By the way, you can have up to 4 graphics cards for an SLI or Crossfire configuration, depending on your motherboard.

For the best gaming performance in every way, it's almost always best to spend your money on one good graphics card. So if you have £100 to spend on graphics, buy one card for £100 (approx. $150 USD), not two at £50 (approx. $75 USD) each. This is the same at every price point. So if you have £600 to spend on graphics, buy one card for £600 (approx. $920 USD), not two at £300 (appox. $460 USD) each.

Obviously, having two graphics cards sometimes makes sense. If you want more graphics power than one card can give you, or you'll be using more than one monitor, two graphics cards may suit you. But most of the time, one good graphics card is better than two inferior cards.

So what about having three or four graphics cards in one PC? Well, I would advise against this. The more graphics cards you have, the more likely you are to run into scaling and driver problems. Also, there are some games that won't benefit from three or four graphics cards as the FPS produced from them are sometimes no better than having two cards.

If you're using two or more Nvidia graphics cards, they will need to be identical. So for example, you cannot use a GTX 770 card with a GT 740 card. This just won't work. By the way, not all Nvidia cards can be SLI'd. Some have no support for SLI and some have support for two cards only, three cards only or four cards. For example, the GTX 750 Ti cannot be SLI'd at all, while the Nvidia Titan X can be SLI'd up to four graphics cards.

When it comes to using two or more AMD graphics cards, you can mix and match a little, or just play it safe and get yourself two or more identical ones instead. Some AMD graphics cards can only be used on their own with no Crossfire support, while other AMD cards can support two way (two graphics cards), three way or four way Crossfire setup.

Help Choosing A Graphics Card

As I've already mentioned, the graphically intense games are the ones that make your graphics card work hard (such as Crysis 3 and Far Cry 4). They will push your graphics card a lot more than the less graphically intense games such as Minecraft. But there are many games out there today that don't require anywhere near the amount of power these big games ask for. So when it comes to choosing a graphics card, it depends on the type of games you want to play and your monitor's resolution.

So for example, if you want to play Crysis 3 in HD (1920 x 1080) resolution with very high game settings, you'll need a GTX 760 or better from Nvidia, or an R9 280X or better from AMD for the game to run fairly smoothly. These graphics cards cost around £150 (approx. $230 USD) each.

If you want to play Crysis 3 at 2560 x 1440 resolution, again with very high game settings, you'll need a Nvidia GTX 970 or an AMD R9 290X for reasonably smooth game-play. These graphics cards cost around £250 (approx. $380 USD) each.

And Crysis 3 at 4K (3840 x 2160) resolution with very high game settings, you'll need a Nvidia GTX Titan X for fairly smooth *game-*

play. This would cost around £750 (approx. $1,150 USD).

But let's suppose you want to play games that are a lot less graphically intense such as World of Warcraft. For very smooth game-play you'll need:

Nvidia GTX 750 Ti at 1920 x 1080 resolution £100 (approx. $150 USD)

Nvidia GTX 760 at 2560 x 1440 resolution £150 (approx. $230 USD)

Nvidia GTX 970 at 3840 x 2160 resolution £250 (approx. $380 USD)

So as you can see, the games that you'll play and the resolution that you play them in will be the determining factors as to which graphics card you'll buy for smooth game-play.

Before you buy a graphics card, do a Google search for your games' system requirements. The recommended system requirements *(not minimum, that's very different)* will recommend a graphics card. That recommended graphics card will most likely give you around 30 FPS at 1920 x 1080 resolution. If you want to play in a higher resolution, or if you prefer more FPS, then go above the recommendation.

Also, you could do a Google search for the game(s) you want to play and the graphics card that you want, to see if you have a good match. Search on YouTube as well, as many people will upload videos to show you how many FPS their graphics card can manage for various games at various resolutions.

Processor (CPU)

The CPU (Central Processing Unit), is also known as the processor. *CPU and processor will be used interchangeably throughout this book*. The processor is the computer's main microchip, often referred to as the brains of the computer. But you could also see it as the boss of the computer as well. It's the brains because it will take in and send out computer data, processing many calculations per second. And it's the boss of the computer because it will tell everything else what to do. No other computer component is allowed to do anything without going through the processor first.

There are two main companies that offer a range of processors for home computers. Those are AMD and Intel. So let's investigate them now.

Intel Processors

At the time of writing, Intel's latest offerings are their 4th, 5th and 6th generation of processors. These consist of Intel Core i3, i5 and i7 processors. These are what they call their mainstream line-up, as most home computer users that use Intel will opt for one of these. They also have a line of *'High End'* processors that are faster, but obviously more expensive. To see what they have on offer today, go to http://www.ark.intel.com

Intel Processor Model Names Explained

Intel's processors have names such as *'Intel Core i7 4790k'* in their mainstream line-up. The first number in the model name is its generation. As you can see from the example here, the Intel Core i7 4790k model is a fourth generation processor. The last three numbers (790 in this case) will give a general idea of its performance. For example, the Intel Core i7 4790k is faster than the Intel Core i7 4770. Intel processors with a 'C', 'K' or 'X' at the end of their model name indicates that they are unlocked (overclockable).

Intel's *'high end'* processors have their own generations. For example, the *'Intel Core i7 5960X'* is a fifth generation Intel processor from their high end line-up.

There are other types of Intel processors such as the Intel Pentium, Celeron and Xeon, but for a home/gaming computer, you'll want an Intel Core i3, i5 or i7 if you're going with Intel.

AMD Processors

AMD's latest processors for gaming computers are called *'AMD FX'*. They do have many

other processors available, but for a gaming computer, you'll want an AMD FX processor, if you're going with AMD. Their latest processors on offer (at time of writing) start with the numbers 95, 93, 83, 63 or 43. For example, the *'AMD FX 6350'* and the *'AMD FX 8370'* are two of AMD's latest processors.

Their previous generation of processors start with the numbers 81, 62, 61 or 41. for example, the *'AMD FX 8150'* and the *'AMD FX 6130'* are two of AMD's processors that are one generation older. For an up to date list of AMD FX processors, go to http://www.amd.com

AMD Processor Model Names Explained

As mentioned, you'll see AMD processors with names such as *'AMD FX 8370'*. The first number of each processor model name refers to how many cores it has (more on cores in a moment). So the AMD FX-4xxx processors have 4 cores, the AMD FX-6xxx processors have 6 cores, the AMD FX-8xxx processors have 8 cores and the AMD FX-9xxx have... er, well, still 8 cores. Naming systems are sometimes a little strange for some computer components.

The second number refers to its generation. So the AMD FX-x5xx and the AMD FX-x3xx are AMD's newer processors, and the AMD FX-x2xx and the AMD FX-x1xx are one generation older.

The last two numbers refer to the CPU's performance. So for example, the FX-8350 is faster than the FX-8320. But remember that newer generations of CPUs are generally better performers, which can throw this theory out a little. For example, the FX-8320 (newer generation) is faster than the FX-8150 (older generation). Also note that some of AMD's processors have an 'E' in their title, for example, the *'AMD FX 8320E'*. The 'E' means that it's an energy efficient processor.

CPU Clock Speeds And Cores

The CPU's speed (called its clock speed) is measured in GHz (Gigahertz). 1GHz = 1 billion cycles per second. So a CPU that has a clock speed of 1GHz will be able to execute 1 billion tiny pieces of data per second. Over the years, CPUs have become faster and faster and still continue to grow in speed today.

To understand the CPU a little more, I want to take you way back in time to around the year 1999. No CPU manufacturer had yet produced a CPU for a home computer that had a clock speed of 1GHz. Then in the year 2000, the 1GHz CPU was available to purchase and marketers made a big deal of it.

Over the years beyond that, CPUs were made that had even faster clock speeds. But the problem is that when a CPU is clocked at around 5GHz, it produces a lot of heat. At that clock speed, the CPU could overheat and stop working. So manufacturers hit a wall.

To continue making faster CPUs, they produced a dual core version. In other words, one physical CPU with two CPUs (known as cores) inside it. Since then we've had a 3 core, 4 core, 6 core and an 8 core version available for home PCs.

A single core CPU (like the ones back in the days of the 1GHz CPUs) can only perform one task at a time. So if you have two programs open at the same time, they would have to share the CPU, resulting in both programs being slower to respond. A CPU with two cores (a dual core CPU) can perform two tasks at a time. So if you have two programs open at once, they can have one core each, resulting in both programs responding faster. Or if you only have one program open, that program may take advantage of the two cores and use them both for itself. Many programs opened at once would have to share the two cores.

CPU Threads (Hyper-threading)

So what is a thread? Well a good way of picturing it is that each program you have open in Windows will be connected to the CPU via a thread (data path).

Most Intel Core i3 processors have four threads and two cores (two threads per core). In this instance, if you have four programs open in Windows, each program will have its own thread (access point to a core). So two programs could share the first core and two programs could share the second core. Shown below.

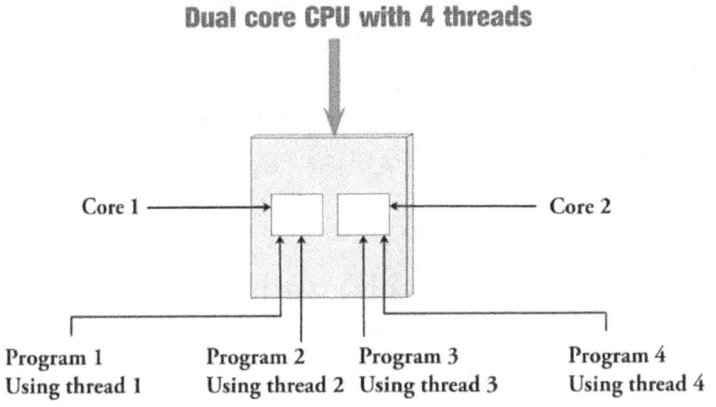

Let's have another example. Many Intel Core i5 CPUs have four threads and four cores (one thread per core). So this time, each thread leads to its own core. So four opened programs in Windows would each have their own thread, and each of those threads will lead to its own core. So no need to share cores in this instance. Shown below.

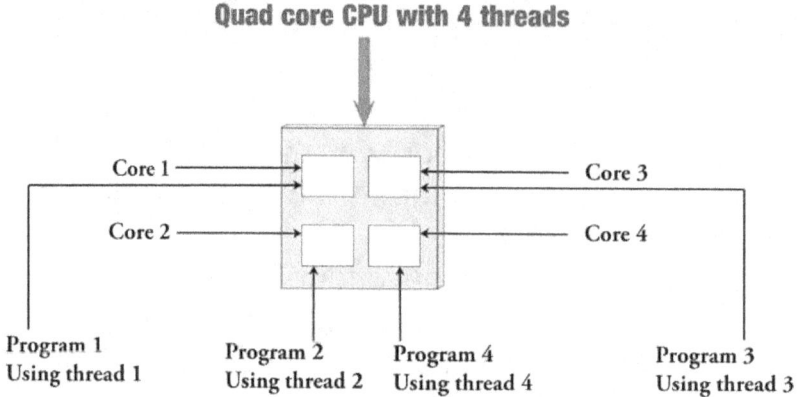

Quad core CPU with 4 threads

Core 1
Core 2
Core 3
Core 4

Program 1
Using thread 1

Program 2
Using thread 2

Program 4
Using thread 4

Program 3
Using thread 3

Extra threads will give a good performance boost to any CPU, but not as much as having extra cores. For example, a CPU with four threads and four cores will be a fair bit faster than a CPU with four threads, but only two cores. Basically it comes down to this... the more cores and threads the CPU has, the faster it will be.

CPU Cache Memory

Every CPU will have its own cache memory (aka CPU memory or CPU RAM). The CPU cache memory is pre-built onto the CPU itself and is used to store frequently requested data. CPU cache sizes are normally measured in KB (Kilobytes) or MB (Megabytes). CPUs can have cache memory level 1 (often written as L1), level 2, level 3 and sometimes level 4 too. The following is an example of this.

AMD FX 8370 CPU's Cache Memory

L1 384KB

L2 8MB

L3 8MB

The larger the CPU cache size is, the quicker the computer will be when it comes to repetitive tasks.

CPU Turbo Speed

Many processors have a turbo speed. For example, a processor may have a normal clock speed of 3.5GHz. But when it needs some extra power, the clock speed will automatically go up a notch or two, to perhaps, say, 3.9GHz. Not all processors have a turbo speed, but most do these days.

AMD vs Intel

The two biggest CPU manufacturers are AMD and Intel. So which one should you choose? Well they both offer some great processors, but I'll give some general advice on both AMD and Intel. Intel have some top-of-the-line processors. They perform better at lower clock speeds (compared to AMD) as they are more efficient. So, let's say, you have a quad core AMD processor running at 3.6GHz and a quad core Intel processor running at 3.5GHz. The Intel processor would get more work done because of its efficiency, even though it has a lower clock speed. Intel also tend to be better when it comes to single threaded performance over AMD's processors.

AMD are better for budget computer builds as their lower priced processors tend to be good performers for the price. So if you're on a tight budget, AMD is the way to go. They also have more overclockable processors, as all of the AMD-FX series can be overclocked.

Help Choosing An Intel Processor

The more cores the processor has, the better. The faster the clock speed, the better. The more threads it has, the better. The larger the CPU cache memory, the better. The newer the generation... the better.

The *'Intel Core i3'* CPUs are the cheapest out of the i3, i5 and i7 from Intel. Most gamers prefer an Intel Core i5, but if your budget doesn't stretch that far, an Intel Core i3 is still a good option.

For many gamers, an Intel Core i5 CPU is just right. Not the most expensive, but still really packs a punch.

The Intel Core i7 processors are more expensive, but obviously, they are the fastest. If you can push the boat out a little, then get yourself one of these. You have a choice between an Intel Core i7 from Intel's mainstream range, or from their high end range. The high end Intel Core i7 processors are more expensive though and would only suit those that have a bigger budget.

Help Choosing An AMD Processor

At the time of writing, the newest generation of AMD FX processors were the FX-x3xx and the FX x5xx. The newer generation of processors are faster, so they'll be better for gaming and general computer use too. The more cores they have, the better. The faster the clock speed, the better. And finally, the larger the CPU cache size, the better.

Processor Cooler

If you buy a boxed processor, it's extremely likely to arrive with a heat sink and fan.

**Boxed Processor With a
Heat Sink And Fan Inside**

Heat Sink and Fan

The heat sink is a block of metal that will sit on top of the processor. The heat sink is used to dissipate the heat from the processor. The fan will sit on top of the heat sink and will blow the hot air away. This is all done to keep the processor from over heating.

If you're *not* going to overclock your processor *(make it run faster than it's supposed to)*, using the heat sink and fan that arrives boxed with the processor will be absolutely fine. If you are considering overclocking your processor, you'll want to get yourself a third party CPU cooler. *If you'll be using the heat sink and fan that's boxed with the processor, you may want to skip to 'System Memory (aka RAM)'*
.

There are two types of third party CPU coolers to choose from... air cooled or liquid cooled. An air cooler normally consist of a heat sink and fan(s) that will sit on top of the processor. A liquid cooler usually consist of a radiator and fan(s) that have tubes connecting them to a block. The block will sit on top of the processor. Both an air cooler and a liquid cooler is shown on the following pictures

There are three things to be aware of, if you do decide to get a third party CPU cooler. The first is that some of them won't fit into some of the computer cases available today. So you'll have to do your homework on that before you buy one. The second is that you'll have to find out your processor's socket type and make sure that your third party CPU cooler is designed for that same CPU socket type. And finally, some third party CPU coolers will not allow you to install tall memory modules. None of this is a concern if you're going to use the heat sink and fan that arrives with your processor. So if I haven't put you off of using a third party CPU cooler at this point, then read on for a few recommendations.

Third Party Heat Sink And Fan (sat on top of a processor and motherboard)

Third Party CPU Liquid Cooler Installed

Help Choosing a Processor Cooler

A very popular third party air cooled CPU cooler is the *'Cooler Master Hyper 212 Evo'*. A very popular third party liquid cooler is the *'Corsair H80i GT'* (smaller radiator) or the *'Corsair H100i GTX'* (larger radiator), though Corsair do make many other popular liquid coolers, some at a cheaper price. There are other companies that also make good quality CPU coolers (liquid and/or air CPU coolers) such as Arctic and Cooler Master.

To overclock a processor, you'll want three things which are:

an unlocked processor
a motherboard that has overclocking features
a third party CPU cooler (ideally)
By the way, overclocking your computer can potentially damage your components and void any warranties.

System Memory (RAM)

Memory and RAM (Random Access Memory) will be used interchangeably throughout this book.

So what is system memory used for? Well, let's suppose you want to do some video editing. You open up a video in your favourite video editing software. The video and the video editor will be copied from the hard drive (where all your programs and files live) and sent to the system memory. The system memory can then send parts of the video to the CPU for processing, as and when needed. This will make editing much quicker because the system memory is much faster at communicating with the CPU, compared to the hard drive communicating with the CPU. Once the program is closed or the computer is turned off, all data from the memory is flushed out. Anything saved beforehand will be stored on the hard drive.

How Much System Memory Is Needed For Gaming?

The simple answer to this question for today's games is about 8GB. If you have the money, go for 16GB which should keep you going for some time to come.

Let me expand on this a little. There are many games out there at the moment that will use around 4GB. There are quite a few graphically intense games that use up to 8GB right now. So for today's games I'd recommend 8GB of system memory, but no doubt, in the near future, some games will require more than this.

Memory Speed

When you go browsing the various memory modules on offer for your new PC, you'll notice that they have a figure next to them, such as, for example, 1,333MHz. This is because, not only do all computer memory modules have a certain capacity measured in

GB, but they also have a speed measured in MHz. The faster the computer memory modules are, the faster they can perform, which can make your computer a little faster.

Each memory module will have a particular DDR technology. Here are the memory speeds that can be achieved with the various DDR technologies

DDR 200 – 533MHz

DDR2 400 – 1066MHz

DDR3 800 – 2133MHz

DDR4 2133 – 4266MHz

So, for example, a memory module with DDR3 technology might have a speed of 1066MHz. One with DDR4 technology might have a speed of 2666MHz. Most will find that memory modules with a speed of 1,333MHz will be fast enough for gaming right now. Most modern motherboards these days will accept either DDR3 or DDR4 memory, but not both.

Single, Dual, Triple And Quad Channel Memory

These days, motherboards have single, dual, triple or quad channel memory technology. So what is this all about? Well, if you have two memory modules installed in a motherboard that has *'dual-channel memory'* technology, both memory modules can push through their data to the CPU at the same time. If you have four memory modules installed in a motherboard that has *'quad-channel memory'* technology, all four memory modules can push through their data to the CPU at the same time. In other words, quad-channel is faster than dual-channel.

Most motherboards that support DDR3 memory modules will have dual-channel memory technology. Motherboards that support DDR4 memory modules are likely to have quad-channel memory technology.

You don't need special memory for this. You know, you're not looking for *'dual-channel capable memory'* or anything like that. The motherboard is the component that will boost the performance of the memory that you install if it has dual, triple or quad-channel memory technology.

If you're browsing for *DDR3 RAM*, you'll notice that they're often sold in pairs. This is because, to take full advantage of dual-channel memory technology, the memory modules need to be identical. So for example, you may see 8GB of RAM being sold as 2 x 4GB. And *DDR4 RAM* is often sold in packs of four, for motherboards that support quad-channel memory.

By the way, you can install however many RAM modules you like into a motherboard that supports single, dual, triple or quad channel memory (up to the number of available motherboard RAM slots). For example, if you have a motherboard with four RAM slots that will also support dual-channel memory, you can install just one RAM module, or three RAM modules if you like. It's just that doing this means that you won't get the full benefit of dual-channel memory speeds, as you would with two or four RAM modules installed.

Latency

When browsing the various memory modules, you'll often see numbers next to them that look something like this: '9-10-9-27' or '16-18-18-35'. These numbers are telling you the memory's latencies (delay times). The CAS latency is the first number of the four. CAS latency is the time it takes (measured in clock cycles) between data being requested from the memory and the memory releasing that data. The lower the CAS latency is, the faster the memory's response times will be (e.g. 9-9-9-27 is faster than 10-9-9-27). The other three numbers are also to do with latency timings (again, the lower the better) but they don't have that much of an impact on memory performance. CAS latency is the one that matters the most. Memory with faster CAS latency timings will be more expensive though as they are more responsive.

Physical Size Of The Memory

When using a third party CPU cooler, the memory modules can sometimes be too tall to fit in-between the motherboard's memory slots and the CPU cooler. This isn't a problem when using an AMD or Intel CPU cooler that arrives boxed with the CPU itself. But sometimes, now and then, it's a problem when using a third party CPU cooler. A way around this, if you do come across this problem, is to use *'low profile'* memory modules which are not as tall and will fit in-between just about any CPU cooler and motherboard.

The reason why some memory modules are so tall is because they have a taller heat spreader. The part of the memory that looks like fins is the heat spreader. This will dissipate heat from the memory module itself.

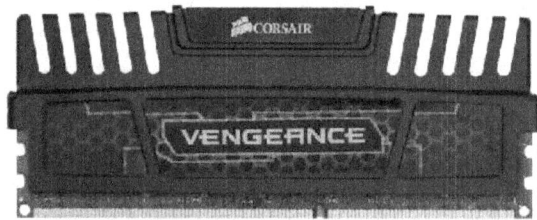

Low profile memory, on the other hand, will have a shorter heat spreader. Because of this, they cannot be overclocked as much as taller memory modules. Well, at least this is true most of the time. But this won't be a problem for those that have no intention of overclocking their memory.

Overclocking any computer component can cause damage to your computer and may void any warranties.

XMP (Extreme Memory Profile)

You may come across certain memory modules that have XMP support. XMP is used to push up the speed of the memory automatically. This is basically an automatic overclock of the memory.

How this works: you can go into the motherboard's BIOS or use motherboard's software and click on an XMP profile. This will automatically push up the memory's speed and set any other settings that also need to be changed such as voltage, memory timings etc. This makes it very easy to overclock the memory. For this you'll need memory and a motherboard that both support XMP. This is not a must have, but can be great for overclockers.

Help Choosing System Memory

There are quite a few memory manufacturers that make good quality memory modules such as Corsair, Crucial, G.Skill and Kingston. The more memory that you have installed, the better, though 8GB – 16GB will be plenty for gamers right now. The faster the RAM speed, the better, though speeds of 1,333MHz should be plenty for most. And finally, the lower the latency, the better. Having XMP is a nice touch too, but not essential.

All modern motherboards will accept either DDR3 or DDR4 memory modules. The memory that you choose has to be compatible with the motherboard. A guide to choosing compatible memory for your motherboard has been written in the *motherboard* section of this book.

Hard Drive

The hard drive will store all of the computer data including programs, games, photos, videos, music and so on. Windows is also stored on the hard drive. The more space the hard drive has, the more programs and files the hard drive can store.

Hard Drive Storage Space

Hard drive storage space is measured in TB (Terabytes), GB (Gigabytes) or MB (Megabytes).

1TB = 1,000GB

1GB = 1,000MB (Megabytes)

Many hard drives these days will have around 500GB – 2TB in space. One game may use under 1GB of space, but some games use or over 50GB, so they do vary a lot. As a guide, for most people, having 1TB – 2TB of hard drive storage space will allow enough room for all the games, photos, music, programs and anything else you want to throw onto your PC.

Hard Drive Speed

Every hard drive will have a speed rating. The speed rating is how fast data can be read from the drive (read speed) and how fast data can be written to the drive (write speed). The read/write speeds of a hard drive are measured in MB/s (Megabytes per second).

So for example, let's suppose you have a game on your computer, or to be more specific, on your hard drive. When you click on that said game to start it up, the hard drive will be read from. If you have a fast hard drive that has a read speed of 500MB/s, the game might start up in, let's say, 30 seconds. But using a slower hard drive that has a read speed of under 100MB/s might mean that that same game will take over 2 minutes to load.

A faster hard drive will give you faster computer start-up and shutdown times, faster game and program loading times and a generally more responsive computer too. *More on hard drive speed coming up.*

Different Types Of Hard Drives

There are three types of hard drives to choose from... those drives are:

HDD (Hard Disk Drive)

SSD (Solid State Drive)

SSHD (Solid State Hybrid Drive)

All of them do the same thing (store data), but all three vary in speed and price. So let's take a look at them individually.

HDD (Hard Disk Drive)

HDDs have been used for many years and are still very much in use today. They are mechanical drives with disks *(called platters)* inside them that spin round. Heads inside the drive will move back and forth over the disks to read data from them and write data to them. They are generally the slowest of the three hard drives, but they're also the cheapest.

SSD (Solid State Drive)

SSDs (Solid State Drives) have no moving parts. They're like a big USB flash drive in the way that they store data on a circuit board housed inside a casing. Because they have no moving parts, they are completely silent and they are, by a long way, the fastest of the three drives, but they're also the most expensive.

SSHD (Solid State Hybrid Drive)

A 'Solid State Hybrid Drive' is often called 'Hybrid Drive' for short, or SSHD as we'll call it. SSHDs have a HDD and a SSD inside them. A typical 1TB SSHD will have a 1TB HDD and an 8GB SSD.

Even though SSHDs have two drives (SSD and HDD) housed inside one physical drive, they are seen by Windows as one hard drive. Files that are accessed regularly are added to the SSD part of the drive automatically. This means that starting up the PC and loading regularly used programs will be done faster compared to using a HDD. The SSHD will automatically store files that don't need fast access to the HDD part of the drive, such as music and photos. SSHDs are a little more expensive than HDDs but are generally a little faster.

Comparing Different Types Of Hard Drives

So let's get some facts on the table so that you can compare the three drives. The two most important things to consider when choosing a hard drive are the storage space and the speed. Well, three things if you include the price. Here are three typical 1TB hard drives for you to compare, just to get an idea.

HDD 1 TB £40 (approx. $60 USD) 120 MB/s average read speed
SSHD 1 TB £55 (approx. $85 USD) 170 MB/s average read speed
SSD 1 TB £240 (approx. $370 USD) 520 MB/s average read speed
SSDs always perform much faster than SSHDs and HDDs. So whether you're loading a game or another program or booting up Windows (and various other tasks), an SSD will perform much faster, all day long.

HDDs are the slowest but can still be great for actual game-play, because here's the thing... games don't need a very fast hard drive. So having an SSD will show little performance benefit to actual game-play. So if you're on a tight budget, get a SSHD or a HDD. If you're not, get an SSD and enjoy a much more responsive PC.

SATA Speeds

Hard drives can have either SATA 1, SATA 2 or SATA 3 technology. A hard drive that has SATA 1 technology (sometimes written as SATA 1.0) can read and write data at up to 150MB/s (Mega Bytes per second). This is sometimes written as 1.5Gb/s. Here are three SATA technologies that a hard drive might have and their read/write speeds.

SATA 1.0 150MB/s (1.5Gb/s)
SATA 2.0 300MB/s (3Gb/s)
SATA 3.0 600MB/s (6Gb/s)

So a hard drive that uses SATA 3 technology has the potential to read and write data to and from the hard drive at 600MB/s. But notice I say *'Potential'*. Not all SATA 3 hard drives are equal in speed. You'll see some HDDs with SATA 3 technology that have a read and write speed of under 100MB/s. But when it comes to SSDs with SATA 3 technology, some will have read and write speeds of over 550MB/s.

So before you buy a hard drive, you may wish to check its read and write speed to see how fast it can actually perform, not just whether it's an SATA 2 or SATA 3 drive. This is obviously not essential but may be of interest to you. When searching for a hard drive, descriptions don't always show you the read and write speeds (also known as the transfer rate). But a quick Google search for the hard drive you're interested in will often reveal professional reviews that will show you the read/write speeds of the drive and much more.

By the way, you'd be hard pushed to find a hard drive that uses SATA 1.0 technology any more. In fact SATA 2.0 drives are also becoming a little scarce too.

All hard drives these days use SATA technology. This means that you'll need an SATA cable for every hard drive that you have (HDD, SSHD or SSD). The SATA cable will attach the hard drive to the motherboard.

Hard Drive RPM Speeds

All HDDs and SSHDs will have an RPM (Revolutions Per Minute) speed rating. In other words, how fast they can spin the disks inside the drive. SSDs don't have an RPM speed rating because they have no disks inside them to spin. Many hard drives can spin their disks at 5,400 RPM or 7,200 RPM. The faster the disks can be spun, the more likely it is that the drive will have faster read/write speeds.

Hard Drive's Cache Memory

HDDs use cache memory (aka buffer size). This is measured in MB (Mega Bytes). So you may see a HDD advertised as having, for example, 32MB of cache memory, sometimes written as '*32MB buffer size*'.

So what is cache memory? The most recently accessed hard drive files will be stored on the hard drive's cache memory. If those files are requested again, they will be accessed from the cache memory. This is a faster way of accessing the most recently used data from the hard drive. The bigger the cache memory, the more recently accessed files it can store. So a HDD with, *let's say*, 64MB cache will be faster than an identical HDD that only has 8MB of cache when it comes to repetitive tasks.

Help Choosing A Hard Drive

There are quite a few HDD companies to choose from. Some of those companies known to make reliable HDDs are Hitachi, Samsung, Seagate and Western Digital. But all HDDs are fragile, so if it's been dropped during shipping or if you've dropped it yourself then it may be damaged or dead already. So the message here is, go careful with it. Some HDDs are faster than others so you may want to seek out one such as the Western Digital Black or Velociraptor *(fast HDDs)* as oppose to a Western Digital green HDD (energy efficient but slower HDD).

The choice for SSHDs are fewer. Companies that make SSHDs are the likes of Seagate and Western Digital. They're not quite so in demand as many people choose to have either a HDD on its own, or an SSD for Windows and a few other programs and games, coupled with a HDD for storing music, photos, videos and so on. But they still make for a good hard drive. *By the way, SSHDs are also quite fragile.*

SSDs are great for speeding up the general speed of your PC. If you can afford an SSD, you'll see your computer boot up, shut down, load programs and games much quicker than any HDD or SSHD ever could. There are quite a few companies that make good quality SSDs such as Crucial, Intel, Kingston, OCZ, Samsung and Sandisk. It's best to pick one that has good read/write speeds as they do vary a lot. A fast SSD would be one that has above 500MB/s read and write speeds.

Optical Drive (DVD Drives and Blu-ray Drives)

Most DVD drives are capable of playing DVD movies, PC games (on a DVD or CD disk) and music CDs. Blu-ray drives can normally do all of the above, but they can also play Blu-ray movies. Optical drives are becoming a little less popular these days as many people are downloading their games instead of buying them on a disk, but they're still very useful to have in case you need one.

DVD Drive Installed In A Computer Case

Since around 2009, all optical drives sold have SATA technology. This means that they have an SATA port that requires an SATA cable. So you'll need one SATA cable for every optical drive that you have. This cable will attach the optical drive to the motherboard.

Help Choosing An Optical Drive

One of the best selling DVD drives right now is the Samsung SH-224DB. It can read and write to DVDs and CDs. It has all the speed you'll ever need and it's quite quiet too all for around £13 (approx. £20 USD). Asus also make great DVD drives. As for Blu-ray drives, the LG BH16NS40 is a great choice. Other good brands for Blu-ray drives are Asus and Pioneer. There are others, but those are my handful of recommendations.

Motherboard

The motherboard is the main circuit board that's used to connect everything else together. Choosing a motherboard has a lot to do with compatibility. Will it take that DDR3 memory that you want? Will it work with the CPU that you've chosen? Does it have enough USB ports for your USB devices? These are the types of questions that come up when choosing a motherboard.

Here are some of the official motherboard manufacturer's websites that you'll find very helpful when trying to find out what each motherboard has to offer.

Asus: http://www.asus.com

EVGA: http://www.evga.com

Gigabyte: http://www.gigabyte.com

MSI http://www.msi.com

Cheap vs Expensive

There are many motherboards out there to choose from at many different price points, so I'd like to take you through what's what. First off, let's start with the price. As you can buy a motherboard for about £40 (approx. $60 USD), or one for around £400 (approx. $600 USD), or anything in-between, you may be wondering why some motherboards are 10 times more expensive. What do you get for paying that extra money? Well, often the more expensive motherboards will use better components, so they're more likely to last for longer. Also, they're more likely to have more overclocking features to overclock the CPU and RAM. And often you can get better overclocks with the more expensive motherboards as they have better cooling for their on board microchips. They may also have extra features such as an easy to flash BIOS and BIOS backup.

So is it worth spending so much more money on a motherboard? Well the simple answer is... no. You can get a reliable motherboard with all the features that you'll possibly ever use (including overclocking if that's your thing) for a lot less money.

For example, the Asus Z97 Maximus VII Ranger motherboard has many overclocking features, it's known as reliable, it's easy to overclock, it supports 4th and 5th generation Intel processors, there's SLI and Crossfire support and it has an easy to flash BIOS among other features, all for £130 (approx. $200 USD). You don't even have to spend that much on a motherboard. Just don't go for a rock bottom priced board as a cheap one will most likely have cheap components that may or may not last for very long.

Motherboard Ports

Every motherboard will have some ports at the back of the motherboard itself. The ports that are available will vary from one board to the next. There's often a few USB 2.0 and 3.0 ports, sound ports that you can plug your speakers into, a LAN port to connect to the Internet via a cable and a PS2 port that can be used for older styled keyboard and mice.

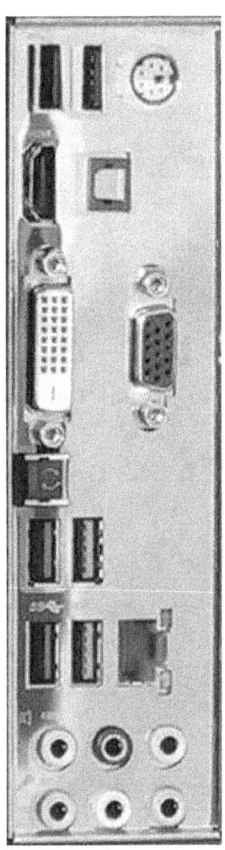

There's also normally some graphics ports too, but you won't be using them as you'll be installing a dedicated graphics card for better gaming graphics. This is a gaming PC you're building after all.

PCI-E x16 Slot

Graphics cards these days are installed into a PCI-E x16 slot on the motherboard. All of the motherboards that have a PCI-E x16 slot (virtually all do) can accept one AMD or one Nvidia graphics card.

PCI-E x16 Slot

Some motherboards have two PCI-E x16 slots and can accept either two AMD graphics cards or two Nvidia graphics cards.

Two PCI-E x16 Slots

So if you're going for two graphics cards, look for a motherboard that has Crossfire support (multiple AMD graphics cards) or SLI support (multiple Nvidia graphics cards).

It's exactly the same for three or four graphics cards. So if you want to throw your money away on that many graphics cards, then at least check that the motherboard you're choosing can support all of those AMD or Nvidia cards.

PCI-E x1 Slot

Most motherboards will have at least one PCI-E x1 slot. These slots are often not needed, but can be useful if you want to add additional cards such as a TV card, wifi card, sound card or something else.

PCI-E x1 Slot

The reason why they're often unused is because all of the features that you normally need are on the motherboard these days. So for example, you're unlikely to need a sound card plugged into a PCI-E x1 slot as most motherboards have on board audio already. So instead of installing a sound card into a PCI-E x1 slot, you can simply plug your speakers into an audio port at the back of the motherboard.

Most motherboards also have a LAN port for you to connect to the Internet via a cable. Some don't have wifi though, so you may need a PCI-E x1 wifi card and a motherboard

that has a PCI-E x1 slot, if you want to connect your PC to the Internet wirelessly.

PCI SLOTS

Before PCI-E slots came onto our motherboards, PCI slots were used instead. PCI slots are much slower than PCI-E slots and are different in their physical size. Just a handful of motherboards can still be found that have one or two PCI slots (alongside PCI-E slots). But PCI technology is completely different to PCI-E, so don't get the two mixed up.

Two PCI Slots (white) And One PCI-E Slot (black)

System Memory Slots

Every motherboard will have a certain number of slots where the memory modules can be installed. The number of memory module slots will vary from one motherboard to the next, but most have two or four slots, some have six or even eight, as shown on the following page.

Each slot can accept a certain amount of memory (depending on the motherboard). So let's say you have a motherboard that has four memory slots and each slot can accept up to 8GB. This would mean that you can install up to 32GB of memory in that motherboard. Also, every motherboard will state very clearly which type of memory it will accept (for example, DDR3 or DDR4).

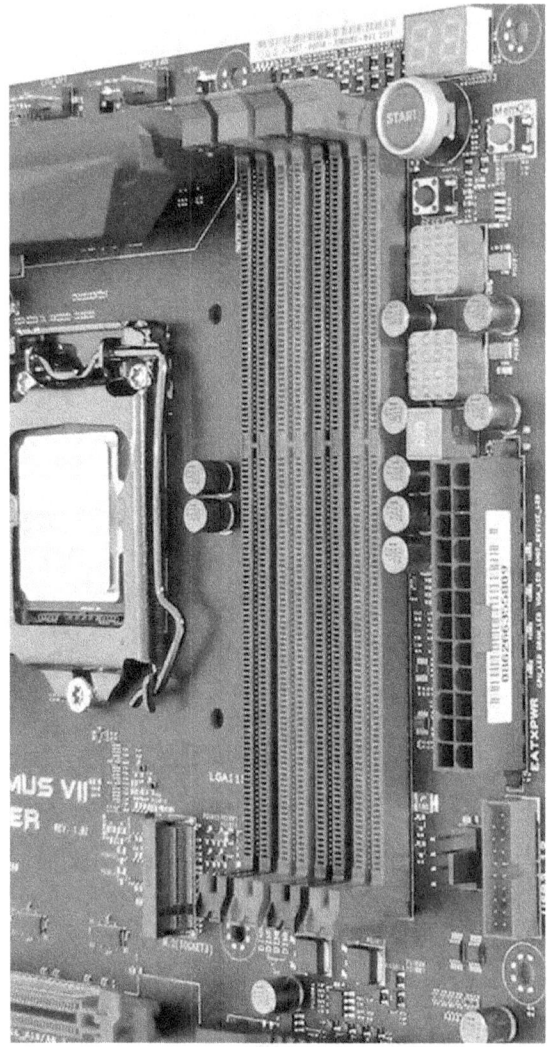

Memory Module Slots

SATA Ports

SATA ports on the motherboard are used for hard drives (including hard disk drives, hybrid drives and solid state drives) and optical drives (including DVD drives and Blu-ray drives). So you'll most likely want a motherboard that has at least two SATA ports so that you can connect your hard drive(s) and optical drive(s) to the motherboard via an SATA cable (one cable per drive).

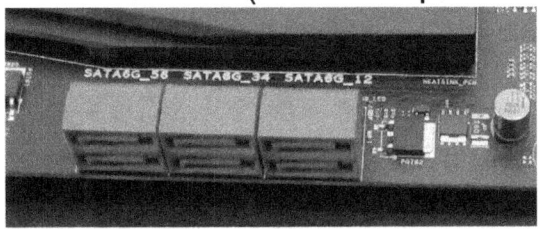

Ideally, look for a motherboard that has two or more SATA 3.0 ports (sometimes written as SATA 6Gb/s ports) to go with your SATA 3.0 hard drive(s). Most motherboards have at least two SATA 3.0 ports these days. By the way, SATA 2.0 and 3.0 are fully backwards and forwards compatible. In other words, you can use an SATA 2.0 or 3.0 hard drive with a motherboard that has SATA 2.0 or 3.0 ports.

Motherboard Sizes

There are quite a few different sized motherboards out there, but I'm just going to talk about the ones that are more commonly used.
EATX motherboards measure up to 330mm width x 305mm height. EATX motherboards are often used for Intel's '*high-end*' processors, but can be used for other processors too. These boards have plenty of room for features such as PCI-E slots and memory module slots.
ATX motherboards measure in at 244mm width x 305mm height and are the most popular among gamers and computer users. They have plenty of room for PCI-E slots and memory module slots.
mATX (micro ATX) motherboards measure 244mm x 244mm. These boards don't have the room for as many PCI-E slots or memory module slots compared with EATX or ATX boards, but they can fit into smaller computer cases.

Mini ITX (aka mITX) motherboards are the smallest out of the boards mentioned here, measuring just 170mm x 170mm. They have even less room for PCI-E and memory module slots and are not used very much by gamers, but they can fit into the smallest of computer cases.

XL-ATX motherboards are a bit of an oddity. They don't really have a standard size, but to give you an idea, they tend to be around 255mm width x 330mm height. They have plenty of room for PCI-E slots and memory module slots too and tend to be taller than all of the other boards mentioned above.

Motherboard's CPU Socket Type

Whichever CPU you choose, it will have a socket type. You'll then need to choose a motherboard that has the same CPU socket type for them to be able to work together. So for example, if you chose an Intel Core i7 4790k (a fourth generation Intel processor), then you'll need a motherboard that has an LGA 1150 CPU socket type. Here are the latest socket types.

Intel's 6th generation processors use an LGA 1151 socket type.

Intel's 4th and 5th generation processors use an LGA1150 socket type.

Intel's 5th generation of *high-end* processors use an LGA 2011v3 socket type.

Intel's 4th generation of *high-end* processors use an LGA 2011 socket type.

AMD FX processors currently require an AM3+ socket type.

Chipsets

The motherboard's chipset will determine which processors the motherboard can support and certain features that the motherboard can have. Yes, that's right, you can't just get a motherboard that has the right socket type for your processor. It has to have the right chipset as well.

Note that the motherboard's chipset is nearly always within the motherboard's model name. For example, the 'Asus Z97 Pro' motherboards have a Z97 chipset.

Intel Chipsets

Here are the latest chipsets (at time of writing) for motherboards that accept Intel processors with some information about each one, starting with the best chipsets.

Intel X99: supports Intel's 5th generation of *high-end* processors. Motherboards using this chipset will also support DDR4 RAM, quad-channel memory and are very likely to have CPU overclocking abilities.

Intel Z170: supports Intel's 6th generation of Intel processors. Motherboards using this chipset will also support DDR3 RAM or DDR4 RAM or both and are very likely to have CPU overclocking abilities.

Intel H170: will support Intel's 6th generation of Intel processors. This chipset was not released at time of writing, hence, no other information.

Intel Z97: supports Intel's 4th and 5th generation of processors. Motherboards using this chipset will also support DDR3 RAM, dual-channel memory and are very likely to have CPU overclocking abilities.

Intel H97: supports Intel's 4th and 5th generation of processors. Motherboards that use this chipset will also support DDR3 RAM and dual channel memory. Most motherboards using this chipset will *not* have CPU overclocking ability.

Intel Z87: supports Intel's 4th generation of processors. Motherboards using this chipset will also support DDR3 RAM, dual-channel memory and are very likely to have CPU overclocking abilities.

Intel H87: supports Intel's 4th generation of processors. Motherboards that use this chipset will also support DDR3 RAM and dual channel memory. Most motherboards using this chipset will *not* have CPU overclocking ability.

AMD Chipsets

AMD's latest chipsets (at time of writing) are called AMD's '9-Series'. This includes the '990FX', the '990X' and the '970' chipset. All three chipsets here support AMD FX processors. If overclocking is your thing, the 990FX chipset is the best one to have for that.

Motherboard Bundles

Just before we get into *'Motherboard and Processor Compatibility'* in the next section, I'd like to tell you about motherboard bundles. Motherboard bundles include a motherboard and processor, and sometimes memory modules are included as well.
Buying a bundle will guarantee compatibility with the processor and motherboard straight out of the box (and the memory as well, if it's included). This is very useful for those that can't be bothered with the whole CPU and motherboard compatibility thing. Many of these motherboard bundles can be found on the Amazon website, among many other websites too.

Motherboard and Processor Compatibility

So you've checked that your motherboard has the right CPU socket type for your processor. You've also checked that your motherboard has a chipset that is compatible with your chosen processor. That's a really great start. But you'll still have to check whether the processor that you've chosen will work with the motherboard that you've picked out. I cannot give you exact instructions on this, as I cannot tell you about every motherboard and every processor and whether they are compatible or not. So I'll have to let you do your homework on this one. Here are some of the motherboard manufacturer's official websites again, which you may find helpful:

Asus: http://www.asus.com

EVGA: http://www.evga.com

Gigabyte: http://www.gigabyte.com

MSI http://www.msi.com

Motherboard and Memory Compatibility

You probably already know how much memory you want to install into your PC by now, but it has to be compatible with the motherboard that you've chosen. This is made easy by various websites that can help you out.

One way of finding memory that's compatible with your motherboard is to go to a memory manufacturer's website such as Corsair at http://www.corsair.com/en-gb/memory-finder for the UK or http://www.corsair.com/en-us/memory-finder for the USA. Once on the website, in the drop-down box where it reads *'Step 1: Select System type'*, you need to select *'Motherboard'*. In the drop-down box below that, select your motherboard manufacturer. Next, in the last drop-down box, select your motherboard's model and click on *'Go'*. You'll then see a selection of RAM that is 100% compatible with your chosen motherboard.

Finding memory that's compatible with your chosen motherboard can be done on other websites too, such as:

http://www.kingston.com
http://www.crucial.com
http://www.gskill.com

Help Choosing A Motherboard

Asus and Gigabyte motherboards have a good reputation for reliability. The Asus ROG (Republic of Gamers) motherboards are very much recommended for those that have a little extra in their budget.

A motherboard with a Z97 or H97 chipset will be best if you're going to use an Intel 4th or 5th generation processor. Motherboards with either of these chipsets will support DDR3 memory.

A motherboard with a Z170 will be best for those that will be using an Intel 6th generation processor. Motherboards with this chipset will support either DDR3 or DDR4, but most likely won't support both. There are other chipsets due to be released for motherboards that support Intel's 6th generation processors (such as the H170), but the Z170 was the only chipset released at the time of writing.

Motherboards with an X99 chipset will support Intel's 5th generation of high-end processors. Motherboards with this chipset will support DDR4 memory.

And finally, a motherboard with a 990FX, 990X or 970 chipset is recommended for AMD processor users. Motherboard features do vary a lot with AMD motherboards, so check that it does have all of the features you want (DDR3 or DDR4, USB 3.0 ports etc.) and that it supports the processor that you've chosen before you buy.

Check the Asus or Gigabyte website for their latest motherboards at http://www.asus.com or http://www.gigabyte.com Some of the other motherboard manufacturers you may be interested in are EVGA and MSI, though there are others on the market as well.

Computer Case

Choosing a computer case partly comes down to personal preference. Do you want a black case, or maybe an orange or a white one? Do you want a small or large case?
Larger computer cases are more likely to hold any computer component you throw in them (I'm looking at you, third party processor coolers). But obviously, larger cases take up more space in your computer den. So let's look at some of the options to help you decide on a computer case that's
right for you.

Case Sizes

There are many different computer case sizes to choose from. Most are similar in shape to the one shown below.

Computer Case

Some cases are short and thin, while others are tall and wide and some are cube shaped. Some PC cases are made to look like something else such as a steam train or Dr Who's Tardis. So how do you pick a case that's right for you? Well let's go through some of the more standard, commonly used cases.

Computer Case	Also Known As	Approximate Case Height
EATX (Extended ATX)	Full Tower	55 –65cm
ATX	Mid Tower	40 –55cm
mATX (micro ATX)	Mini Tower	30 –40cm
mITX (mini ITX)	Small Form Factor	20 –30cm

E-ATX: E-ATX cases will accept E-ATX motherboards. These cases are the largest of the four mentioned above, often measuring around 55 – 65cm in height. These cases are
often used for those that want two, three or four graphics cards installed, as these larger cases have more room. They also typically have around five optical drive bays and eight to ten hard drive bays. Some E-ATX cases can also accept ATX, mATX, mITX and XL-ATX motherboards.

ATX: ATX computer cases will accept ATX motherboards. These cases are a little smaller than E-ATX cases often measuring about 40 – 55cm in height. They are the most popular case size for gamers right now. Many consider this case size to be just right as they often have enough room for all that you want to throw in there without being too big. They normally have enough space for two graphics cards, two to four optical drives and four to eight hard drives. Some ATX cases can also accept mATX and mITX motherboards.

mATX: mATX cases will accept mATX motherboards. These cases are a little smaller than the ATX cases with an approximate height of 30 – 40cm. They often have room for one graphics card, one or two optical drives and two to four hard drives. You can build a good gaming PC in these cases but you would have to choose your computer parts carefully as they are not as spacious as E-ATX or ATX cases. Some mATX cases can also accept mITX motherboards.

mITX: mITX cases will accept mITX motherboards. These cases are the smallest of the four mentioned above coming in at around 20 –

30cm in height. They often have room for one graphics card, one optical drive and a couple of hard drives. These cases are the least popular with gamers as they are so small, but you can still build a good gaming PC with one of these if you choose your parts very wisely. The mITX cases can only accept mITX motherboards as they're not big enough to accept any of the other motherboards mentioned above.

The names that manufacturers and retailers give to their case sizes (full tower, mid tower, mini tower or small form factor) are just a guide. For example, most full tower cases will accept E-ATX motherboards but some will not. Most mid tower cases will accept ATX motherboards but some will not. So names such as full tower, mid tower, mini tower and small form factor can be a little misleading. To make sure you get the right case for your motherboard, see which motherboards the case will accept before you buy.

Cheap vs Expensive Cases

Let's get straight to the point in this section as little explaining is needed. Cheap computer cases will sometimes have slightly sharp edges inside the case, so you may have to watch yourself a little with that. They also tend to be less solid, less sound proof, have less vibration dampening and with less areas for cable management. The more expensive cases tend to be the opposite of this, often having no sharp edges, a more solid construction, better sound proofing, more vibration dampening and grommets or holes for cable management.

There's absolutely nothing wrong with buying a cheap case if that's what you want. Having a cheap case won't make your computer go any slower. So if you don't mind what's just been mentioned, then a cheap case is fine to use. If you have a little extra in your budget, you might appreciate a better quality computer case.

Case Fans

Most computer cases have pre-installed fans inside them.

Pre-installed Case Fans

This often consists of a fan or two at the front, and one at the back. They are nearly always designed to pull air in from the front of the case, and blow air out at the back. These fans help to keep everything inside the computer case cool enough so that nothing will overheat.

There's four things that can really heat up inside the computer case which are, a HDD, an SSHD, the graphics card and the processor (especially an overclocked one). The fan(s) at the front of the case will help keep a HDD or an SSHD running cooler. Graphics cards that need extra cooling will have their own fans. Processors have there own fans too. All of the hot air that accumulates inside the computer case is blown out at the back of the case and/or out of the top.

As a guide, if you have one processor, one HDD or one SSHD and one graphics card inside your computer case and you're not going to overclock your computer, you should *not* need to install any extra fans inside your computer case, (assuming your computer case has at least one fan pre-installed at the front and back). By the way, it's OK to have a few SSDs because they work at low temperatures. It's HDDs and SSHDs that can get quite hot.

So let's say you have one graphics card, one hard disk drive and two SSDs inside a computer case that has a pre-installed fan at the front and back. And of course you'll have all the other parts in there too such as the motherboard, memory, perhaps a wifi card, a DVD drive and so on. The air flow that's created by the fans inside the case should be good enough to keep everything running at reasonable temperatures so that nothing will overheat.

So when do you need extra case fans? Well, you may need an extra fan or two if you have more than one graphics card and/or more than one HDD or SSHD and/or you'll be overclocking your computer. This isn't always the case, but you might need extra cooling in those situations. Extra case fans can be installed at the front, bottom, side, back and top of the computer case, though some cases don't offer all of those options. As a general rule, any fans installed at the bottom, front and side of the computer case should be pulling air in, and any fans installed at the back and top of the case should be blowing air out.

Cooling isn't an exact science though. For example, I cannot tell you that if you have two graphics cards, you'll need *xx* fans at the *xx* part of the case. But using this section as a guide should see you right.

If you're going with two graphics cards, it's best to buy a motherboard that has a reasonable amount of space in-between the PCI-E x16 slots. This will keep the graphics cards separated from each other and therefore they'll be much less likely to overheat. Many computer cases have a place for 80mm, 90mm, 92mm, 120mm and/or 140mm fans. Some cases can hold a larger fan and some can hold smaller fans, but these are the most popular fan sizes for cases available today. Some computer cases have more than two fans pre-installed already to save you the bother of installing extra fans, if that's what you need.

Extra Information

Some of the older cases that are still available today don't have a place to store a solid state drive. So if you want to use an SSD, make sure the case you choose has a place to hold one.

Check that your case has enough room for your graphics card(s) as some of them are quite long and won't fit in all sized cases.

If you're getting a third party CPU cooler (for overclockers), make sure there's room for it as some cases are not big enough for some of the larger third party CPU coolers. CPU coolers that arrive boxed with the CPU itself will always fit into any case.

Help Choosing a Computer Case

Computer case manufacturers, Corsair and Fractal Design, make some really good computer cases. Some of the very popular ATX cases include the *Corsair 230T*, the *Corsair 200R* and the *Fractal Design Define R5*. A popular E-ATX case that could be used is the *Corsair 750D*. All of the cases mentioned here have lots of room for long graphics cards, places for SSDs, USB 3.0 ports at the front and at least one fan at the front and back of the case. The Corsair 750D case will also accommodate most of the longer CPU liquid coolers (radiators) such as the Corsair H100i. There are plenty of good computer cases out there. The ones I've mentioned here are just a few recommendations to help you on your way.

PSU (Power Supply Unit)

The PSU (often referred to as the power supply) is used to power up all of the computer components inside the computer case. It's also used to power up some of the external devices as well. For example, an external USB hard drive that doesn't have its own power source (it's not plugged into the wall) will be using power from the power supply. As the power supply is used to give life to so many components, there's no doubt that it's an important part of the computer build.

Power Supply Inside A Computer Case

Cheap vs Expensive Power Supplies

Do NOT buy a cheap power supply! Here's why... a cheap power supply will often have little to no safeguards such as over current and over voltage protection. Also, they often only have a one year warranty and tend to stop working after about a year and a half. When they do malfunction, they're more likely to kill your other PC components at the same time.

A good power supply on the other hand will often have many safeguards such as:

OVP (Over Voltage Protection)

UVP (Under Voltage Protection)

OCP (Over Current Protection)

OPP (Over Power Protection)

OLP (Over Load Protection)
OTP (Over Temperature Protection)
SCP (Short Circuit Protection)
They will also have good warranties (often 3 to 7 years) and are very unlikely to ruin other PC components if they do develop a problem. So the message here is clear... don't buy a very cheap power supply.

Efficiency

All power supplies vary in how efficient they are when using power from the wall. Some waste more power than others which will give you a higher electric bill and some waste less which will lower you're electric bill in comparison.

Most power supplies these days have a power efficiency rating. These ratings are shown next in order, starting with the most efficient.

Power Efficiency Ratings

80 Plus Titanium
80 Plus Platinum
80 Plus Gold
80 Plus Silver
80 Plus Bronze
80 Plus

The '80 plus' rating at the bottom of the list is the least efficient, but this is still better than a power supply with no rating at all.

The upsides to getting an efficient power supply are:
- You'll save some money on your electric bill
- They generate less heat which means less fan noise
- They're likely to last for longer

So are there any downsides to getting one of these power supplies? Well, the more efficient a power supply is, the more it will cost you to buy in the first place. So it's good to get a balance that's right for you.

Power Supply's Physical Size

An ATX power supply will have a standard size of 15cm width and 8.6cm height (or at least very close to that measurement). But their depth will vary, often between around 14cm – 16cm. An ATX power supply should be used with an ATX or E-ATX computer case. mATX power supplies also have a standard size of 15cm width and 8.6cm height (or at least very close to that measurement). But the depth can vary, often between about 10cm – 13.9cm. A mATX power supply should be used with a mATX computer case. Some mATX cases can also accept an ATX power supply, but not all can, so stick with a mATX power supply for a mATX case if you're uncertain.

A mITX computer case will use a small form factor power supply such as a mITX, SFX, TFX or a mATX. All mITX cases and small form factor power supplies vary in size, so check before you buy, if this is what you're going with.

Power Connectors

Attached to the power supply itself will be many cables. At the end of these cables will be various power connectors. These connectors are used to give power to the components inside the computer case such as the motherboard, hard drive, DVD drive and so on.

Next are the power connectors you'll come across on most power supplies, along with a description for each one.

24 pin Motherboard power connector (Shown above)

This connector is used to give power to the motherboard. Most motherboards these days need a 24 pin power connector as shown in the picture (2 rows of 12 pins). Some use a 20 pin connector instead. By the way, many power supplies will be advertised as having a 20+4 pin connector. This means that it has 4 detachable pins so that it can be used as a 20 pin or a 24 pin power connector to power the motherboard.

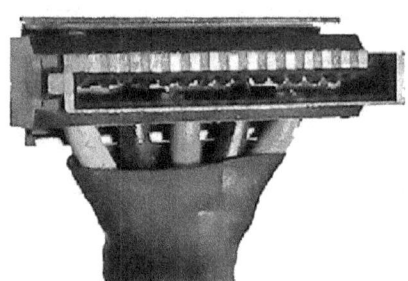

SATA Power Connector (Shown above)

These connectors are used to give power to hard drives (including hard disk drives, solid state drives and hybrid drives) and optical drives (including DVD drives and Blu-ray drives). The amount of SATA power connectors a power supply will have, will vary.

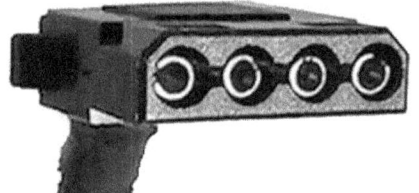

4 Pin Peripheral (aka Molex) power connector (Shown above)

These connectors were used a lot more years ago, but are not used very often today. They were used for hard drives, optical drives, some dedicated sound cards, case fans and various other components. It's unlikely that you'll need one of these for a new computer build today, but they are still used now and then and are included with almost all power supplies.

Floppy (aka mini Molex) Power Connector (Shown above).
This connector is used to power up a floppy disk drive. I don't know of anyone that still has a floppy disk drive any more. They were very popular years ago but they're never installed in computers today. But this power connector is sometimes still used for other PC components such as various card readers and a few dedicated sound cards. As this power connector is so rarely used in modern computers today, it's sometimes not included at all with some power supplies.

6 Pin PCI-E Power Connector (Shown above)

8 (6 + 2) Pin PCI-E Power Connector (Shown above)
These power connectors are used to give power to the graphics card. The graphics card that you buy may need no PCI-E power connectors, or it may need one or two 6 or 8 pin PCI-E power connectors. The graphics card that you want should clearly state

what it needs. One *'6+2 pin PCI-E power connector'* can be used as a 6 pin or an 8 pin PCI-E power connector.

CPU Power Connector (Shown below)

These power connectors are used to give power to the CPU (you plug them into the motherboard). Most motherboards these days will use either an 8 pin CPU power connector (described as an *'EPS 8 pin 12 volt'* power connector), or they may use a 4 pin CPU power connector (described as an *'ATX 4 pin 12 volt'* power connector). Most power supplies have both, as the EPS 8 pin 12 volt power connector can often also be split into two, to give you two *'4 pin ATX 12 volt'* power connectors.

Modular vs Non-Modular

When using a modular power supply, it's possible to detach all of the cables from the power supply itself. A semi-modular power supply is one that has some detachable cables and a non-modular power supply has all of its cables permanently attached to it.

The advantage of a modular power supply is that you only need to install the cables that you need for your PC. This will allow for better air flow inside the computer case, keeping everything a little cooler.

The advantage of a non-modular power supply is that you don't have to figure out where each cable should be plugged in (into the power supply), though this is normally fairly obvious. Also, you'll never lose any of the spare cables.

It doesn't matter whether you choose a modular or non-modular power supply. It really just comes down to which you prefer.

Silent And Near Silent Power Supplies

Many power supplies have a fan inside them. The only noise you'll ever hear from a power supply (excluding coil whine that some suffer from) is its fan spinning round.

In an effort to try and reduce noise from the power supply, many manufacturers are now designing them so that the fan will only spin when needed. If you're interested in a power supply like this, look out for ones that are advertised as having a 'Zero RPM Fan Mode' or 'Fanless Mode' or something along those lines. Some models don't even have a fan which make them completely silent all of the time. Those fanless power supplies are often used for media centre computers though and are not used so much for gaming computers.

Voltage

Here in the UK, our mains electricity is rated at 230 volts. So if you live in the UK, get yourself a power supply that is rated at 230 volts. Other places may vary, so check that the power supply you're buying has the right voltage rating for your country or area. Some power supplies have a voltage selector so that the voltage rating can be chosen by you, simply by moving a switch on the power supply itself.

How Many Watts (Wattage)?

When choosing parts for a PC, you should always choose the power supply last (not including the monitor). This is because you need to know how power hungry the computer components that you've chosen will be.

So first off you'll need to work out how many watts your new computer will use. To do this, you can use a 'power supply calculator' online. You can Google this, or just use one that I personally recommend which is http://outer-vision.com/power-supply-calculator by *eXtreme Outer Vision*. Click on the *'Expert'* tab near the top of this website before you start.

Next, enter the computer parts that your new PC will be using into the drop-down boxes. If you're going to overclock your processor, use the sliders for your overclocking amount. Next, click on 'Calculate'. You will then be given a recommendation on how many watts your power supply should have as shown on the next picture. Whilst the *'Recommended PSU wattage'* will be enough for your computer build, most prefer to add between around 50 – 100 watts to the total just in case of an upgrade in the near future such as an extra hard drive, more USB devices etc. I would recommend this to err on the side of caution.

Load Wattage: **392 W**

Recommended UPS rating: **750 VA**

Recommended PSU Wattage: **442 W**

	Amperage (combined)	
+3.3V	+5V	+12V
8.1 A	12.4 A	25.3 A

Recommended Power Supply:

EVGA 600 B1 80+ BRONZE, 600W 3 Year Warranty Power Supply 100-B1-0600-KR

amazon.com

Calculate   Reset

Example Of The Power Supply Calculator's Results

Note that the results not only show you how many watts your new power supply should have, but also how many amps it should have as well on the +3.3 volt rail, the +5 volt rail and the +12 volt rail. Take note of the amount of amps they recommend for your new power supply, ready for the next section.

How Many Amps (amperage)?

Once you've used the eXtreme Outer Vision website for its power supply calculator *(as mentioned in the previous section)*, the results on the website will show you how many amps your computer will potentially use on the +3.3 volt, +5 volt and +12 volt rails.

Amperage (combined)

+3.3V	+5V	+12V
8.1 A	12.4 A	25.3 A

Example Of Amps Results (From The PSU Calculator)

When you're browsing for a power supply, each one should state how many amps it can produce on the +12 volt rail. Some will also show how many amps it can produce on the +5 volt, +3.3 volt and -12 volt rails as well. But it's the *+12 volt rail* that we're interested in here. If the power supply calculator that you've used recommends a power supply that can produce, let's say, 24 amps on the +12 volt rail, then look for a power supply that can produce 24 amps or more on the +12 volt rail.

Here are some websites that you may find helpful when trying to discover how many amps each power supply can produce on the +12 volt rail.

Antec	http://www.antec.com
Cooler Master	http://www.coolemaster.com
Corsair	http://www.corsair.com
Seasonic	http://www.seasonic.com

To keep this simple, go for a power supply with a single +12 volt rail. What do I mean by this? Power supplies with two or more +12 volt rails will have a description such as this:

+12V no.1 = 18 amps, +12V no.2 = 20 amps.

Unless you know what you're doing, go for a power supply that has just one +12 volt rail. Some power supplies that have a single +12 volt rail are recommended next. By the way, if you are going to use a modified graphics card (for example, you buy an overclocked graphics card, such as the Asus GTX 980 Ti OC edition) then you may need more watts/amps than is recommended by the power supply calculator.

Help Choosing a Power Supply Unit

The latest Cooler Master V450, V550, V650 and V750 power supplies are excellent (they are all within the semi-modular series). They all have a 5 year warranty, great build quality and are highly likely to have all the power cables you'll need. The V750 has four PCI-Express cables allowing up to two graphics cards and the others mentioned here have two PCI-Express cables allowing one graphics card. By the way, they are all single +12 volt rail power supplies. Some of the other reputable power supply brands are Antec, Corsair and Seasonic.

Monitor

First we had CRT monitors (those ones that took up lots of space on a desk). Then along came LCD and LED flat screen monitors offering wide screen options and anything from small screen sizes up to very large.

Flat Screen Monitor

But there's lots of variations in size, picture quality and even the speed of the monitor to consider. So I'm going to take you through the most important specifications of a monitor to help you choose one.

Monitor Screen Size

Choosing a monitor screen size is very much a personal choice. Screen sizes are measured from the bottom left corner of the screen, to the top right corner. The most popular screen sizes right now are 19 – 30 inches.

Aspect Ratio

The most popular aspect ratios for monitors are 4:3, 16:9, 16:10 and 21:9.
So what is aspect ratio? Well, the first number (4, 16 or 21) refers to the width of the screen and the second number (3, 9 or 10) refers to the screen's height. So for example, a monitor screen that has a 4:3

aspect ratio has a width of 4 units and a height of 3 units. In other words, for every 4 units in width, there will be 3 units in height.
The 4:3 aspect ratio monitor screens are the ones that look quite square. These are more commonly found in work environments.
The 16:9 aspect ratio monitor screens are the ones that look more rectangular and are called 'Wide Screen'. These are the most popular among home/gaming computer users.
The 16:10 aspect ratio monitor screens are similar to the 16:9 wide screen monitors, but with a little extra height.
The 21:9 aspect ratio monitor screens are the ones that have a width that's approximately double its height and are called 'Ultra Wide Screen'. These can be good for those wanting more work space, and for watching movies without the black bars appearing at the top and bottom of the screen.

Resolution

Every image on a monitor screen will be made up of dots, known as pixels. The more pixels there are to make up a picture, the clearer the image will look. An example would be a 'Full HD' monitor that has 1920 pixels across its width and 1080 pixels up its height. This is its resolution. So a *Full HD* monitor's resolution is described as 1920 x 1080.
There are many different monitor resolutions with many different names. Here are some of the most popular:

Resolution Name	Resolution	Aspect Ratio
XGA	1024 x 768	4:3
WXGA	1366 x 768	16:9
Full HD	1920 x 1080	16:9
WQHD	2560 x 1440	16:9
UWQHD	3440 x 1440	21:9
UHD (4K)	3840 x 2160	16:9

The most popular monitor resolution right now is Full HD. Monitors using this resolution will show good image detail, without bringing a fairly decent graphics card to its knees.

LCD vs LED

An LED monitor is actually an LCD monitor. Let me explain. Both LCD and LED monitors use LCD technology at the front of the monitor screen. The only difference between the two is the back lighting. LCD monitors use CCFL (Cold Cathode Fluorescent Lamps) for their back lighting, where as LED monitors use LED lights for their back lighting.

LED back lighting will help produce better blacks onscreen and better image quality overall. Also, because LED back lighting uses up less space compared with CCFL, LED monitors are generally thinner than LCD monitors. LED monitors use less power too.

There are two types of LED back lighting. The first is LED edge lighting. LED edge lighting uses LEDs around the edge of the panel for back lighting, with a reflective surface behind the whole panel to distribute the light. They use less power because the only backlighting used will be around the back edge of the panel.

The second type of LED back lighting is LED true (aka full array) back lighting. LED true back lighting can offer better local dimming for better blacks and better contrast overall. This will also generally give a better picture quality over edge lighting.

LCD monitors are generally cheaper than LED monitors. LED monitors that use edge lighting are cheaper than LED monitors using true back lighting. At the end of the day, you get what you pay for. If you can push your budget up a little, I would recommend going for an LED monitor, especially as you'll probably upgrade your monitor less often than your other computer parts.

Response Times

A monitor's response time is how long it takes for each pixel to change its colour. This is measured in ms (milliseconds). Fewer milliseconds is better. For example, 2ms is better (faster) than 16ms. So how does this affect gaming? Well, if you have a monitor with a response time of 32ms, you'll find that when you move your character around in a game, using perhaps a mouse, keyboard or gamepad, there will be a delay before you see it move on the screen. It won't be much of a delay, but this can be irritating in a fast paced game. Also, monitors with slow response times have more potential to show blurring or ghosting.

There are many monitors out there today that have a response time of 1ms or 2ms which will give you unnoticeable delay times between you pressing the fire button and seeing your enemy being destroyed on screen. So 1ms or 2 ms response time is ideal for a gamer. 4ms or 5ms response time is still very good, but don't go for anything slower than this if you're really into gaming. At 8ms response time, you may notice a slight difference in very fast paced 'shoot-em-up' games, which could make the difference between hitting a moving target and just missing it.

Brightness

A monitor's brightness is measured in cd/m² (Candelas per square metre). The higher the number, the brighter a monitor can be. For example, a monitor that can produce, let's say, 400 cd/m² can have its brightness turned up higher than one with 200 cd/m². Monitors with a brightness of between 250 – 300 cd/m² will suit just about everyone, accept those that use their computer in a *very* brightly lit room. By the way, monitor brightness can always be turned down if needed.

Viewing Angles

Some monitors have a tight viewing angle. In other words, if you're not sat straight in front of the monitor, but instead you're viewing the screen from the left or right, up or down from the centre, the screen can look darker and the colours start to look a little strange. Some people won't be bothered about this as they're always more or less sat straight in front of the monitor. Monitors can have a viewing angle of up to about 178° (up and down, left and right). So if this is something that concerns you, look for a monitor with wide viewing angles. The wider they are, the better.

Refresh Rate

Most monitors have a 60 Hz refresh rate. This means that if the graphics card is pushing out 60 frames per second, the monitor can display those 60 frames per second on the screen. This will give you a very solid looking game play. Some monitors can produce 120Hz or more. This is more ideal if you're playing games in 3D (you know, with 3D glasses and the like).

Contrast Ratio

Contrast ratio is the difference between the darkest of blacks to the brightest of whites that a monitor screen can produce.

There's two different ways that contrast is measured. The first is normal contrast ratio and the second is DCR (Dynamic Contrast Ratio). A monitor that has its contrast measured will normally have a figure such as 600:1. Where as one measured in DCR will have a figure such as 50,000,000:1. However the monitor has its contrast measured, the higher the number, the better it will be for producing better contrast.

Glossy vs Matte

The difference between glossy and matte monitors is the coating applied to the screen. When using a Glossy screen, images look more vibrant. The downside to using a glossy screen is that they can reflect light sources from within the room. If a reflection of a light is directly on the screen, it can make it virtually unusable. But with little-to-no light reflections, it can look great.

Matte monitors on the other hand will defuse most light source reflections on the screen, but colours may be very slightly dulled. This is not a case of, one is better than the other.

It really comes down to which one suits you the most.

TN vs IPS Monitor Panels

All monitors have a panel (screen) type. The most popular panel type for gamers right now are TN (Twisted Nematic) and IPS (In-Plane Switching).

TN panel monitors are cheaper than IPS panel monitors. TN panels can have a response time of 1ms, but monitors that use an IPS panel don't come that fast. The difference between TN and IPS panel's response time used to be massive, but the gap is getting closer with some IPS panels now having a response time of 5ms or less.

The main advantage of IPS panels over TN are their colour reproduction. The colours on an IPS panel look better, richer, more accurate. The price of IPS panels have come down too, making them closer to the prices of TN panels. And the viewing angles are often much better on IPS panels too.

So which should you choose, TN or IPS? Well, many TN panels now display great looking colours, but IPS panels are still better in that department. Many IPS panels now have fast response times, but TN panels can be faster. Many gamers still choose a monitor with a TN panel for fast paced gaming. But unless you're always playing shoot-em-up games needing super accurate hair-trigger shooting, then you'll probably prefer an IPS monitor (one with decent response times though). There's no clear winner here, it's really a matter of choice.

Monitor Controls

Just about all monitors have controls for brightness, colour, sharpness etc. Often when you first plug in a new monitor, it can look quite bad, with brightness way too high, colour settings off and so on. A quick play around with the monitor controls (and possibly the graphics card's control panel) can rectify this.

If you're struggling to get your monitor colours correct, you can use a free colour calibration tool that comes with Windows 10, 8.1 and 7 called 'Calibrate Display Color'. This will help you set your monitor's brightness, contrast, gamma, colour and will help give you clearer text on screen.

G-Sync

When playing a game on a computer, the graphics card will send a frame to the monitor and the monitor will display that frame. This happens many times a second. But sometimes, the graphics card and monitor become out of sync. For example, the graphics card may be sending 73 FPS to a 60Hz monitor that can only display 60 FPS. This can cause half of the screen to display the previous frame and the other half displaying the new frame at the same time. This is called 'screen tearing' as it looks like the game has been torn in half on-screen. If the screen tearing is really bad, the screen can look torn many times over.

To resolve screen tearing, V-Sync can be turned on, either in the graphics control panel or in the game settings. But turning on V-Sync can cause two other new problems which are stuttering caused by missing frames, and lag (delay between mouse/keyboard or gamepad movement and onscreen movement). G-Sync will eliminate tearing and minimise stuttering and lag, giving you the best of both V-Sync on and V-Sync off.

These days, all computers and monitors can use V-Sync, but not all can use G-Sync. If you want to use G-Sync, you'll need a Nvidia GTX graphics card from the 700 or 900 series, and a G-Sync monitor (some of the Nvidia GTX graphics cards from the 600 series will also support G-Sync). Yes, you have to have a G-Sync monitor as well if you want to take advantage of this newer technology. These monitors have a special chip inside them making them capable of being G-Sync enabled.

This isn't a must have for everyone though. Some gamers don't mind putting up with a small amount of screen tearing, even though it's not ideal. Not only that, there are many games that don't suffer from this problem on many computers. Also, turning on V-Sync will resolve screen tearing, often with no noticeable stuttering or lag. G-Sync monitors are more expensive than monitors without this technology. So be prepared to pay more for your monitor, if this is what you want. G-Sync is very good though and is worth the extra premium if you can afford it.

So to have the whole G-Sync thing, you'll need a Nvidia graphics card that can support G-Sync, a monitor that can support G-Sync, and an up to date graphics card driver.

Currently, G-Sync can only be accomplished over DisplayPort, so don't try to set it up over HDMI, DVI or a VGA connection.

FreeSync

FreeSync is AMD's equivalent to G-Sync. FreeSync will eliminate tearing, while minimising stuttering and lag. For this you'll need a compatible AMD Radeon graphics card that also has a DisplayPort connection, a FreeSync monitor with *'DisplayPort adaptive sync'* and an up to date AMD graphics card driver. FreeSync is currently only supported over a DisplayPort connection.

Monitor Reviews

Reading the specifications of a monitor is very helpful, but reading reviews online, in magazines or where ever else you find them will give you a better all round picture of the monitor in question. For every monitor, there are user reviews and quite often professional reviews too. So have a read of what others are saying about a monitor before you buy, or better still, go and see one working in a shop if you can.

Choosing a Windows Version

Let's start by talking about an older operating system in the name of Windows XP, and work our way up to the latest version, Windows 10.

The oldest operating system mentioned here is Windows XP which is not supported by Microsoft any more so is therefore susceptible to attacks (viruses and the like). So Windows XP is not an option for your new PC build.

Windows Vista is still supported by Microsoft but it's quite out of date now, so I would advise against it for a new computer build. Support for Vista ends on 11th April 2017.

Windows 7 is still a very popular operating system among many computer users. Most of the time, Windows 7 home computer users opt for *'Windows 7 Home premium 64 bit'.* There are other versions such as Windows 7 Professional, but this is not required for a gaming PC.

The thing that most people like about Windows 7 is that it has a classic start menu (unlike Windows 8.1). This makes it easier to see at a glance which programs you have installed on your PC.

Windows 7 is like a polished up version of what Windows Vista should have been with most of the good parts left in and most of the bad taken out. Windows 7 is supported by Microsoft until 14th January 2020.

Windows 8.1 is still very widely used. *'Windows 8.1 Pro'* is another option, but is not required for a gaming PC. The thing that some like about Windows 8.1 is the layout of apps on the screen. The apps are laid out as tiles on the desktop screen. They look much more like they're designed to be used with a touch screen tablet rather than a desktop PC but can be used with either. One thing to note is that Windows 8.1 has better built-in security for anti-virus straight out of the box compared to Windows 7. Windows 8.1 is supported by Microsoft until 10th January 2023.

Some people don't like Windows 8.1, but some do. When it comes to gaming on Windows 8.1 verses Windows 7, it really doesn't make any difference. If you're very into social media, you may prefer Windows 8.1 with some media updates shown at a glance. But even though it's an older operating system, many people still prefer Windows 7 with its more traditional layout.

Windows 10 is an operating system that fairly much combines the best of both Windows 7 and 8.1. There are several versions of Windows 10 including Mobile, Education, Home, Professional and Enterprise. You'll want the *'Home'* version for a gaming PC, unless you're using your computer for business as well, in which case *'Professional'* might be more appropriate for you.

The full start menu is back and well laid out so that you can easily see what's installed on your computer. The start menu can also be resized in Windows 10 which is a new feature. Apps appear next to the start menu, which is more user friendly compared to Windows 8.1 which somewhat separates the apps and start menu screens.

Cortana is another feature of Windows 10 that acts as a personal assistant. Cortana will help you find things on your PC, track packages, and even chat with you if you wish.

Windows Hello will allow you to login using your fingerprint (fingerprint scanner needed) or your face (webcam needed). Or you could just use a password to login instead.

There's a new Windows store for Windows 10 where you can download apps for your computer. There are pre-installed built-in apps too with this operating system.

The *Search* feature has improved a fair bit compared to Windows 7 and 8.1 as well. Simply type into the search box and your programs, apps, files, folders, Windows and the web can be browsed based on your search words.

As a gamer, you may be interested to know that if you have an Xbox, you'll be able to stream games from your Xbox to your computer if you're using Windows 10. It's like having an Xbox inside your computer and playing Xbox games on your PC screen. Support for Windows 10 ends on 14th October 2025.

All Windows support end dates are subject to change.
Windows 10 can be purchased on a USB flash drive from many retailers such as Amazon.

Windows 10 (USB Flash Drive Inside The Box)
There are 64 bit and 32 bit versions of Windows 7, 8.1 and 10. All motherboards and processors for desktop computers sold today are 64 bit. To complete the package, you'll want a 64 bit version of Windows such as *Windows 10 Home 64 bit*.

Extra Bits Needed For Your PC Build

Once all of your computer parts have arrived, you'll probably have all the cables, screws, odds and ends that you'll need to build your new PC. But let's go through what you do and don't need, just to be sure.

SATA Cables: these cables are needed for internal hard drives and DVD or Blu-ray drives. Boxed motherboards will often have anything from one to four SATA cables in with them. Sometimes a DVD drive or hard drive may have one boxed with it. If you find that you don't have the amount of SATA cables needed for your computer, you can purchase these cables individually. They can be purchased for around £1 (approx. $1.50 USD).

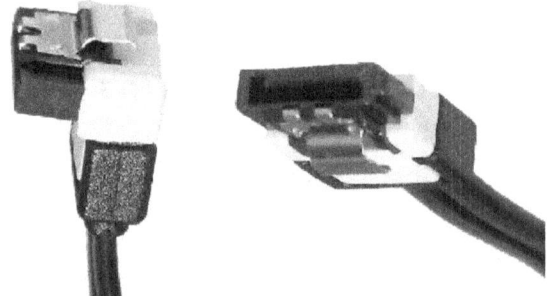

Right Angled SATA Data Cable (Shown above)   SATA Data cable (Shown above)

Front Panel Connector Cables: these are the cables that lead from the front of the computer case (USB ports, sound ports etc.) to the motherboard. These cables come with the computer case as they are permanently attached to it.

CPU Paste: CPU paste (thermal compound) will have to be applied in-between the CPU and the CPU cooler. Often the CPU cooler will have paste pre-applied to it. Or, paste may arrive boxed with the CPU cooler. In these cases, there's no need to buy any CPU paste. Otherwise, you'll need to buy your own. CPU paste isn't very expensive though, so it won't break the bank.

CPU Paste In A Syringe (Shown above)

Power Supply Cables: these all come with the power supply.

Case Screws: these come with the computer case and sometimes other components too.

Motherboard Stand-offs: these also come with the computer case, if they're needed.

Bridge: a bridge is used to connect two or more graphics cards together (not always needed). Often the motherboard will have at least one bridge boxed with it. If not, these can be found online at a fairly cheap price. *You won't need a bridge at all if you're only installing one graphics card.*

Nvidia Bridge (Shown above)

Screwdriver: a screwdriver doesn't arrive boxed with anything, so you'll need one to build your PC. This is most likely the only tool you'll need. A medium sized Phillips (crosshead) screwdriver will do the job.

Extra Case Fans: most computer cases have pre-installed fans (often one or two at the front and one at the back). If you're *not* going to overclock your computer and you're only using one graphics card and one HDD or one SSHD, it's extremely unlikely that you'll need any extra case fans. Some people like to buy extra LED fans that light up the inside of their case just to make it look good. Fans can be purchased on their own reasonably cheaply.

Case Fan (Shown above)

CPU Cooler Backplate and Brackets: these come with the CPU cooler, if needed.

USB 3.0 to 2.0 converter cable: if your computer case has USB 3.0 ports at the front, but your motherboard only has USB 2.0 headers, you'll need a USB 3.0 to 2.0 adapter cable to join them up. This is very often not needed as most modern motherboards have a USB 3.0 header and most modern computer cases have USB 3.0 ports.

Wifi Card: some motherboards have on board wifi, but many don't. So if you want to connect your computer to the Internet wirelessly, you'll most likely need a PCI-E wifi card (can be installed into a PCI-E x1 slot on the motherboard). Just about all motherboards have on board Ethernet (a LAN port), so you can connect your PC to the Internet via a cable. So you don't have to buy a wifi card if you don't mind using a cable to connect your computer to the Internet. Otherwise, get yourself a motherboard with on board wifi, or buy a wifi card.

Sound Card: Nearly all motherboards have on board audio. In other words, you don't need to get a dedicated sound card to hear audio from your PC speakers. Some dedicated sound cards can make your audio clearer though. They normally have more sound options too. So for those that want the best sound quality, a dedicated sound card is the answer. A good quality sound card is the *'Creative Sound Blaster Z'* if you're interested. Most people are very happy with on board sound though.

How To Build A Gaming Computer

Building a PC doesn't take as long as you might think. Start some time the morning and you should have your computer completely up and running before the end of the day, Windows installed and all. If I could give you some general advice, it would be this... take your time with it and don't force anything. If something won't easily connect, it's probably the wrong way round or in the wrong place, so don't use excessive force. Also, handle all circuit boards by their edges. Don't touch the actual circuitry as this can cause problems on the circuit board itself.

This guide will show you how to build a computer using the parts shown below.

Processor: Intel Core i7 4790k
Motherboard: Asus Maximus VII Ranger
Memory: Corsair Vengeance 16GB (2 x 8GB)
Graphics Card: Nvidia GeForce GTX 970 / GTX 980 / GTX 980Ti / GTX Titan X
Case: Corsair 230T
Power Supply: Cooler Master V650
HDD: Western Digital 2TB
SSD: Sandisk 480GB
DVD Drive: Samsung SH-224DB
CPU Cooler: Corsair H80i GT

As you can see from the list shown, I've mentioned four different graphics cards. This is because this computer will accept any one of them. Obviously, this PC will accept other graphics cards too, but I'm showing you how to build a great gaming computer, so I've gone with some great graphics cards that are compatible with this PC. This computer can also accept two graphics cards, but using two would likely mean that you would need a more powerful power supply. I'll also be showing you how to install an Intel CPU cooler (the one that arrives boxed with the processor) as well as the *Corsair H80i GT* shown in the list above, so that you can see how both are installed.

Grounding Yourself

You've probably heard of static discharge. This is where a static charge will build up on your person and is then transferred to something else. For example, you walk across a carpet, building up static within you. You then touch a metal object and a spark briefly appears between your finger and the object. This is static electricity transferring between you and the object and can sometimes hurt a little too.

The trouble is that if this happens when building a computer (static transfers from you to a circuit board), that static discharge can, at worst, ruin a computer component. So you'll need to ground yourself every so often to stop this from happening. To ground yourself, you could use an anti-static wrist strap. If you don't have one, you could instead ground yourself by touching something (for about 10 seconds) that's metal and connected to an earth such as an unpainted tap or an unpainted part of a radiator. Once you've earthed yourself, try not to walk across any carpeted areas as this will, once again, build up some static electricity within you.

Computer Case

Now we can make a start on building a gaming computer. Take your computer case and put it on a table or desk. From the back of the case, take off the right side panel that's held on by a screw.

Side Panel Of Case Removed (Shown above)

Take out the brown box of screws and any documentation you find inside the case.

Installing the DVD Drive

At the front of the case, there are some optical drive bays.

Any of these bays can be used for a DVD or Blu-ray drive, but the top bay is the most commonly used. Now take out a front bay cover (they're clipped in from inside the case).

Optical Drive Bay Cover Coming Out (Shown above)

Take the DVD drive and make sure it's the right way up, then install the drive into the drive bay from the front of the case and clip it into place using the pre-installed clip at the side.

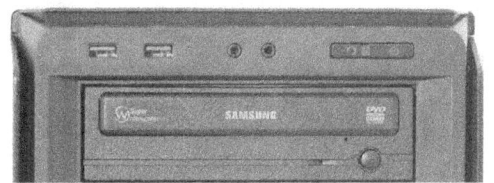

DVD Drive Installed (As above)

Clip For The DVD Drive (As above)

Installing The HDD (Shown above)

Take the HDD and install it into a hard drive bay. You'll need the drive's SATA connections to be facing away from you. Make sure the HDD clicks into place as you gently push it in.

HDD's SATA Connections (Shown above)

HDD Being Installed (Shown above)

HDD Installed (Shown above)

Installing The SSD (As above)

Take your SSD and install it into an SSD bay, just above the HDD bays, with its SATA connections facing the back of the computer case.

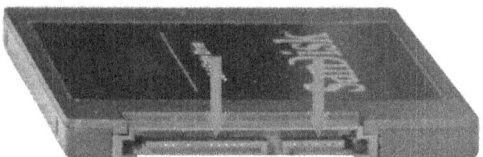

SSD's SATA Connections (Shown above)

SSD Being Installed (SATA Connections Arrowed) (As above)

SSD Installed (Shown above)

Motherboard's I/O Plate

Take the I/O plate out of the motherboard's box.

Motherboard's I/O Plate (Shown above)
This can be installed at the back of the computer case. From inside the case, push the I/O plate into the cut-out. Give it a firm push to make sure it snaps into place all the way around its edges.

I/O Plate Installed (Back Of Case) (Shown above)

Installing The CPU

We're now going to install the processor into the motherboard. You are remembering to ground yourself regularly, right? OK, then we'll carry on. Take the motherboard out of its protective bag and lay it down onto something that is stable but not too hard, such as the motherboard's box.

Next, find the CPU socket on your motherboard.

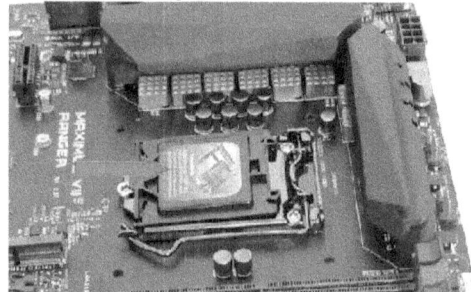

Motherboard's CPU Socket (Shown above)

Lift the metal arm and gently push up the socket's lid.

CPU Socket's Metal Arm Up (Shown above)

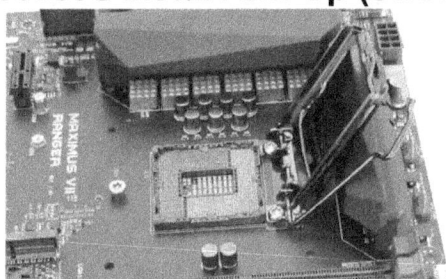

CPU Socket's Lid Up (Shown above)

Take the processor out of its box, remembering to only hold it by its edges. The motherboard's CPU socket and the CPU itself will both have a triangular arrow on one of their corners. You can line up those arrows and install the CPU that way round. So line up your CPU with the motherboard's CPU socket and gently place it down. It doesn't need to be pushed in. Just sit it down in the socket.

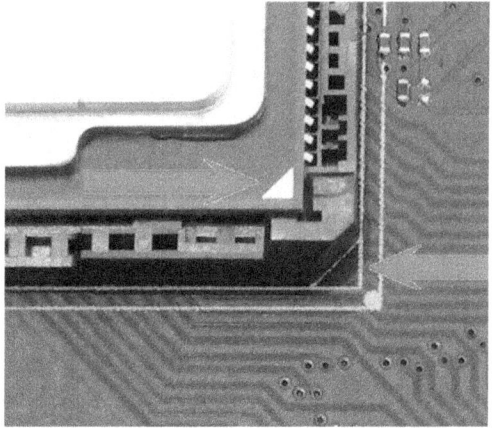

CPU And Motherboard's Triangular Arrows Lined Up (Shown above)

CPU In The Motherboard's Socket (Shown above)

Now push the lid back down making sure the bottom of the lid falls under the motherboard's screw, as arrowed below.

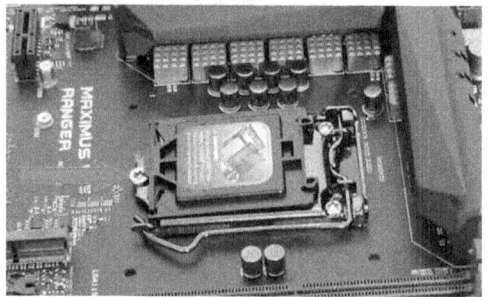

CPU Socket's Lid Down (Shown above)

Push the metal arm back down beside the CPU and secure it into place. The plastic top will pop off by itself as you push down the arm.

CPU Installed (Shown above)

You can put the plastic lid to one side as you won't be needing it for the rest of this build. Don't throw it away though in case you need to return your motherboard for any reason.

Installing The Memory

The memory modules will be installed into the motherboard's memory slots.

Empty Memory Slots On Motherboard (Shown above)

The memory modules can be installed into the red slots on this particular motherboard. These memory slots have a tab at the top of them. They simply need to be pushed open.

Red Memory Slot Tabs Opened (Shown above)

The memory modules have one small cutout along its gold connectors. This needs to be lined up with the notch in the motherboard's memory slot. If it doesn't line up, you have the memory module the wrong way round.

Memory Module Orientation (Shown above)

Once its lined up, push the memory module into the slot on the motherboard. The tab at the edge of the memory module will click into place by itself. The second memory module can be installed in the same way as the first.

Two Memory Modules Installed (Shown above)

Installing The Intel CPU Cooler

If you'll be using the *Corsair H80i GT* to cool your CPU, then skip this part and move on to *'Installing The Motherboard'* as the Corsair H80i can be installed later on. If instead, you're going to use the Intel CPU cooler that came boxed with the CPU itself, then carry on right here.

Intel CPU Cooler (Shown above)

To install the Intel CPU cooler, the four corner pins (as arrowed) need to be turned clockwise by 90° (if they haven't been already).

Just to avoid any confusion, the four pins normally have arrows on them, as shown on the next page. Those arrows are for uninstalling the cooler, so don't turn them that way.

Arrow On Intel CPU Cooler's Pin (Shown above)

The CPU cooler should have some thermal compound (CPU paste) on the cooler itself. It's the grey paste in the middle, as shown below. This will have been applied at the factory, so you don't have to do it yourself. Just check that it's on there and make sure you don't accidentally rub it off.

Intel CPU Cooler's Paste (Shown above)

You'll see four holes on the front of the motherboard around the CPU socket.

Four Holes Around CPU Socket (Shown above)

The four pins on the Intel CPU cooler need to be lined up with those four holes on the motherboard.

Installing The Intel CPU Cooler (Shown above)

Once lined up, push the pins into the holes. The best way is to push two pins in at a time (top right and bottom left, then top left and bottom right). The pins will go through the motherboard holes and will stick out of the other side. You should hear them click into place. After you've pushed in the pins, check the other side of the motherboard to see that the pins have come through properly.

Plug the fan cable connector (arrowed) into the CPU fan header at the top of the motherboard marked 'CPU FAN'. The connector on the cable will only plug in one way round, so don't try to force it on the wrong way round.

Intel CPU Cooler's Fan Cable Connector (Shown above)

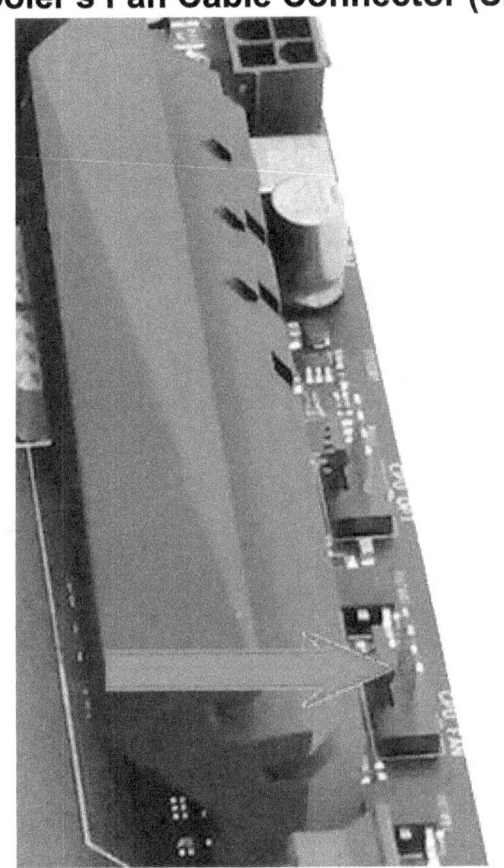

CPU Fan Header On The Motherboard (Shown above)

Installing The Motherboard

Most computer cases use small metal stands, called stand-offs. These stand-offs are used for the motherboard to sit on.

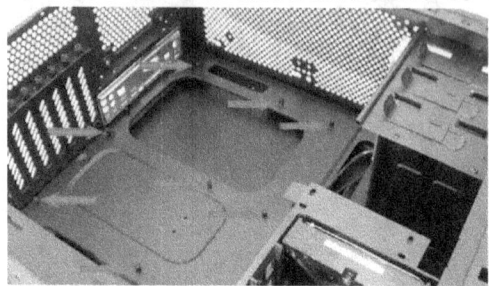

Stand-Offs Inside The Computer Case (Shown above)

The motherboard's ports on the side of the motherboard (shown next) need to line up with the motherboard's I/O plate that was installed earlier into the back of the computer case.

Motherboard Ports (USB Ports, Sound Ports etc.) (Shown above)

You can then sit the motherboard down so that it will be resting on the stand-offs.

Motherboard Installed (Shown above)

I had to take out one of the stand-offs because it did not line up with a screw hole on the motherboard. So make sure there are stand-offs only where your motherboard has a screw hole. You may have to take the motherboard out again to see if they all line up. The stand-offs simply unscrew if you need to take one or two of them out. This is an important step because if there is a stand-off where there is no screw hole on the motherboard, the motherboard may then have a short circuit. So don't skip this step. Check and double check.

Motherboard Coming Out (Again) (Shown above)

Once you've removed any stand-offs that don't line up with a motherboard screw hole, line up the motherboard's ports with the I/O plate once again. Then place the motherboard down onto the stand-offs and screw the motherboard down (screws go into stand-offs). Don't screw them too tightly though as you won't want to crack the motherboard. Just screw them in so that the motherboard is firmly in place.

Screwing Down The Motherboard (Shown above)

Cable Management
This computer case that we're using has holes at the back side of it. Any of these holes can be used to thread cables through so that the cables are kept tidier. This will also help give a stronger airflow

through the case, which means lower temperatures for your computer components. That's why it's a good idea to use them.

Computer Case Holes For Cable Management (As above)

Installing The Front Panel Connectors
At the front of the computer case that we're using, there's a power switch, reset switch, power LED light, hard drive LED light, USB ports and audio ports (microphone and headphone ports).

Front Of Computer Case Ports And Buttons (As above)
Inside the case, there are cables leading from them that need to be plugged into the motherboard (shown next).

Cables Attached To Front Of Case Ports And Buttons (As above)

The cables for the power switch, reset switch, power LED light and hard drive LED light can all be plugged into the Q-Connector that arrives boxed with the motherboard.

Q-Connector (Shown From Three Angles) (As above)

Here's how to plug those cables onto the Q-Connector on both sides.

Cables Plugged Into The Q-Connector (As above)

Next, the Q-Connector can be plugged onto the pins at the very bottom right corner of the motherboard. It will only plug in one way so you can't get it wrong.

Motherboard Pins For Q-Connector (As above)

Q-Connector Installed (As above)

Now let's get those USB ports at the front of the computer case connected to the motherboard. Using your motherboard manual, find out where your motherboard's USB 3.0 header is located. Take your USB 3.0 connector and notice that one of the pin holes is blocked. That needs to be lined up with the missing pin in the USB header on the motherboard.

Missing Pin On USB 3.0 Header (As above)

USB 3.0 Header And Connector (As above)

USB Connector Plugged In (As above)

Now for the audio connector. Check your manual to see where your audio connector should be plugged in on the motherboard. Look at your audio connector and notice that one pin hole is blocked. That needs to be lined up with the missing pin in the audio header on the motherboard (arrowed).

Audio Pins (marked AAFP on the motherboard) (As above)

HD Audio Connector (Shown above)

Audio Connector Plugged In (Shown above)

Installing The Power Supply

Install the power supply into the bottom rear of the computer case, as shown below, then screw it into place.

Power Supply Installed (Shown above)

Power Supply Being Screwed In (Shown above)

By the way, when you get to the stage of turning your computer on, make sure air can get through to the power supply's fan at the bottom of the case. You don't want the power supply overheating after all your hard work.

Now we can install the power supply's power connectors. All of the power connectors can be plugged in one way only. So if you're struggling to push in a power connector, you've probably got it the wrong way round.

Now take one of the SATA power cables that arrived boxed with the power supply.

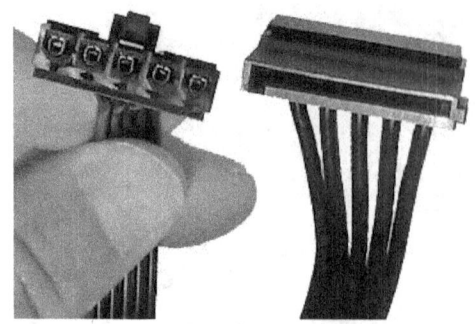

SATA Power Cable (Shown above)

Plug one end of the cable into the power supply (as arrowed) and the other end into the back of the solid state drive.

Ports For SATA Power Cables (Shown above)

SATA Power Cable And SSD (Shown above)

Take another SATA power cable from the power supply's box. Plug one end into the power supply (as arrowed) and the other into the hard disk drive.

Ports For SATA Power Cables (Shown above)

SATA Power Cable Plugged Into The HDD (As above)

Take one more SATA power cable from the power supply's box. Plug one end into the power supply (as arrowed) and the other into the DVD drive.

Ports For SATA Power Cables (As above)

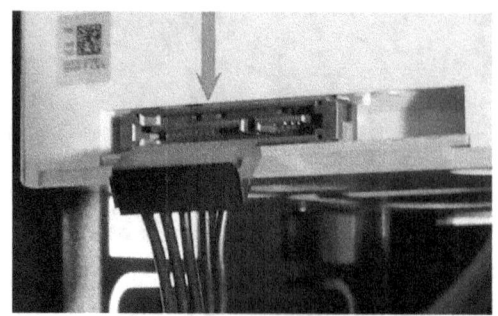

SATA Power Cable And DVD Drive (As above)

Next we can install the connector that will give power to the processor. One thing to note here... the power supply has three 8 pin power connectors. The ones labelled *PCI-E* or *PCI-Express* are for the graphics card (which we'll get to later on). Do *not* plug a PCI-E power cable into the motherboard. Take the other 8 pin power connector (the 8 pin CPU power connector) and plug it into the CPU power port at the top left of the motherboard.

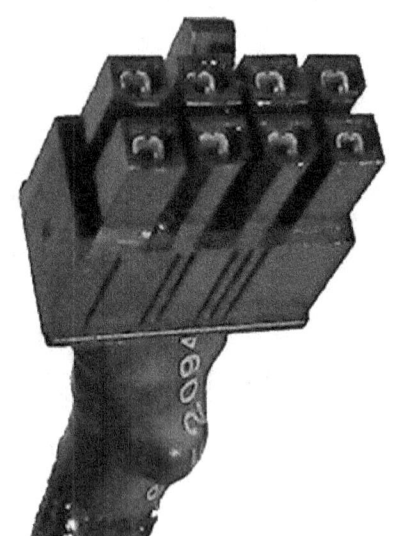

CPU Power Connector (As above)

CPU Power Connector Plugged Into The Motherboard (As above)

Now take the 24 pin power connector and install it into the motherboard (right hand side, middle of the motherboard). It can be a little stiff even when you have it the right way round, but try not to bend the motherboard. Hold the motherboard by its very edge to stop it from bending if you have to. Don't be heavy handed with it.

Motherboard Power Connector (As above)

Motherboard Power Connector
Plugged Into The Motherboard (As above)

SATA Data Cables

Both hard drives and the DVD drive will need an SATA data cable inserted into the back of them. The SATA cables have an 'L' shaped connector, so it can only be plugged in one way.

SATA Data Cable (Shown above)

Take out three SATA data cables from the motherboard's box. Plug one into the back of the HDD, one into the back of the SSD and one into the back of the DVD drive.

SATA Data Cable Plugged Into The HDD (Shown above)

SATA Data Cable Plugged Into The SSD (Shown above)

SATA Data Cable Plugged Into The DVD Drive (Shown above)
The other end of those cables need to be plugged into the SATA
ports on the motherboard. Use your motherboard manual if you're
uncertain as to the whereabouts of your motherboard's SATA ports.

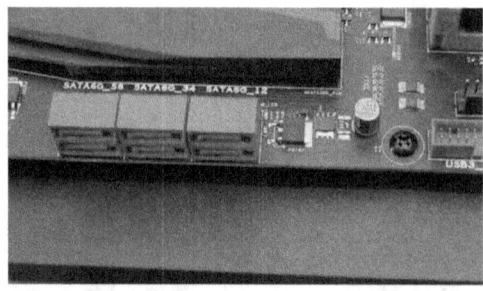

Motherboard's SATA ports (Shown above)

SATA Data Cables Plugged Into The Motherboard (Shown above)

Installing The Corsair H80i GT (CPU Liquid Cooler)

If you've already installed an Intel CPU cooler, skip to the next section *'Connecting The Computer Case Fans'*. If you're installing the Corsair H80i GT, continue right here.

Unscrew the pre-installed fan at the back of the computer case to make room for the Corsair H80i GT radiator and fans.

Back Case Fan Coming Out (Shown above)

Install the Corsair H80i GT's backplate onto the back of the motherboard (Shown below)(other side of the CPU socket).

Back Of The Motherboard (As above)

Backplate Installed (As above)

From the front of the motherboard, install the four screws (shown below) into the backplate.

Screws To Be Used (As above)

One Screw Installed (three to go) (Shown above)

So let's stop for a moment and see what the end result should look like when the Corsair H80i GT has been fully installed.

CPU Cooler (Corsair H80i GT) Fully Installed (Shown above)

A fan needs to be installed on both sides of the radiator. Both fans need to be blowing in the same direction, otherwise they will cancel each other out. The fans should both blow air towards the back of the computer case. There are arrows on the fans so that you'll know which way the fans will blow when turned on and which direction they will spin.

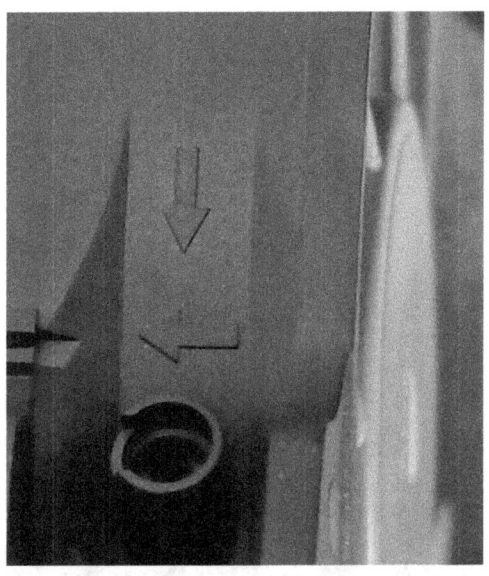

Arrows On The Fan (Shown above)

OK, so back to where we left off. Screw one of the Corsair H80i GT's fans onto the radiator with the tubes facing you. This first fan should be blowing air towards the radiator. *By the way, the fans are identical so you can use either one.*

Fan Screwed Onto The Radiator (Shown above)

The cooling block should have some pre-applied grey thermal paste. Just make sure it's on there and that you don't rub it off.

Cooling Block's Thermal Paste (Shown above)

Place the cooling block onto the processor with the tubes on the right hand side and screw it down.

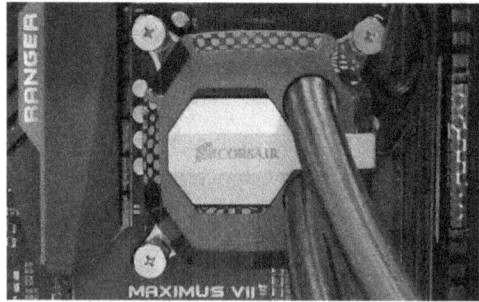

CPU Cooler Block Screwed On Top Of The Processor (Shown above)

Now take the second fan that came with the Corsair H80i GT and place it at the back of the computer case (where you just removed the pre-installed case fan). This fan needs to be blowing air out of the case.

Second CPU Cooler Fan Installed (back of computer case) (Shown above)

Hold the radiator up next to the second fan. Four screws need to go through the second fan and into the radiator from the back of the computer case.

Radiator Installed Onto The Second Fan (Shown above)

The two fans either side of the radiator will have one cable each. And the block that's now screwed onto the processor will have a cable dangling down as well.

Corsair H80i GT Cables Dangling Down (Shown above)

Plug the two fan cables into the CPU block's cable connectors.

CPU Cooler's Fans Plugged Into CPU Block's Cable (Shown above)

That will leave one connector still unused on the CPU block's cable. That connector can be plugged into the motherboard header marked *'CPU FAN'*.

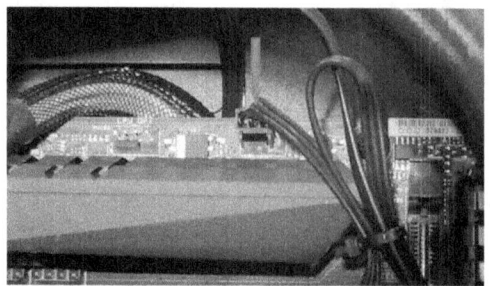

Corsair H80i GT Plugged Into The Motherboard (Shown above)

Connecting The Computer Case Fans

The two case fans at the front of the computer case need to be plugged into the motherboard.

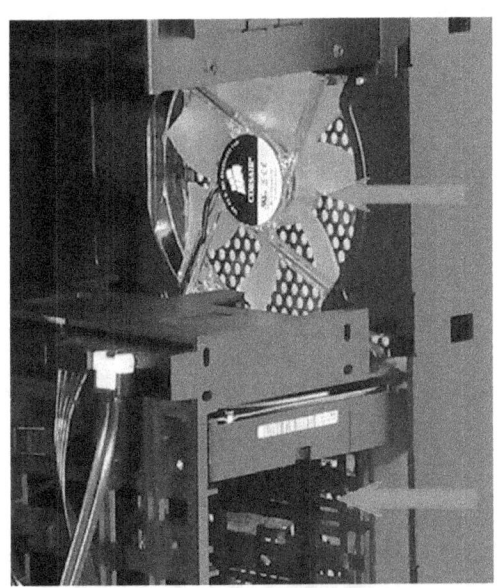

Two Front Case Fans (one mostly hidden) (Shown above)

Plug the bottom front case fan into the header on the motherboard marked *'CHA_FAN 1'*. This header is near the bottom right corner of the motherboard.

Bottom Front Case Fan Plugged Into The Motherboard (Shown above)

Plug the second front case fan into the header on the motherboard marked *'CHA_FAN 2'*. This header is in the middle of the motherboard on the right hand side.

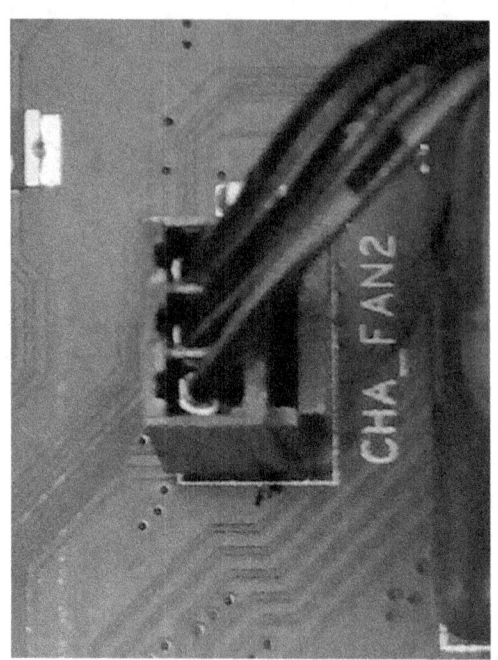

**Second Front Case Fan Plugged Into
The Motherboard (Shown above)**

If you've installed the Corsair H80i GT as your CPU cooler, you can now move on to the next section *(Installing The Graphics Card)*. If instead, you've used the Intel CPU cooler, continue right here.

The back case fan can be plugged into the motherboard header marked *'CHA_FAN3'*. This header can be found in the middle of the motherboard on the left hand side.

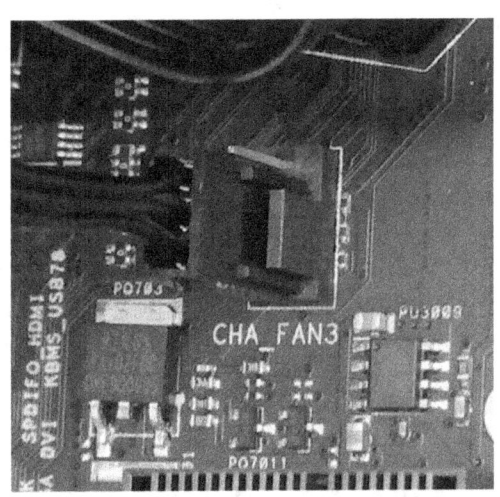

Back Case Fan Plugged Into The Motherboard (Shown above)

Installing The Graphics Card

The graphics card will be installed into the top PCI-Express x16 motherboard slot. As usual, check your motherboard manual if you're not sure which slots are which. Take your graphics card and hold it up roughly where it will be installed (the top PCI-E x16 slot). Notice that three of the brackets at the back of the computer case will need to be taken out. Counting from the top, take out brackets 2, 3 and 4.

Removing Three Brackets (Shown above)

Take off any packaging from the graphics card.

Graphics Card Packaging Coming Off (Shown above)

Next, install the graphics card into the top PCI-Express x16 slot on the motherboard and screw it into place. Bracket number 4 can then be reinstalled afterward.

Graphics Card Installed (Shown above)

The graphics card will need power directly from the power supply. The graphics card shown below requires one 6 pin and one 8 pin PCI-Express power connector.

Graphics Card's Power Ports (Shown above)

Now take a 6 pin and an 8 pin PCI-Express power cable from the power supply and plug it into the graphics card's power ports.

6 Pin PCI-E Power Connector 8 (6 + 2)   Pin PCI-E Power Connector (Shown above)

6 And 8 Pin Power Connectors Plugged Into The Graphics Card (As above)

If you've chosen a different graphics card to the one shown above, you may need some other combination of power. For example, you may need two 6 pin PCI-E power connectors, or perhaps two 8 pin

PCI-E power connectors. If you've chosen one of the graphics cards mentioned earlier (Nvidia GTX Titan X, GTX 980Ti, GTX 980 or GTX 970), the power supply in this PC will have all the PCI-E power cables your graphics card could possibly need. It will also support most other graphics cards too (one graphics card only with this power supply).

Corsair link Cable

The *'Corsair link'* cable can be used so that should you wish to, you can change the performance of the Corsair H80i GT's fans from within Windows 10. The software to enable this is free to download at Corsair's official website (http://www.corsair.com). You can also check the CPU temperature and change the colour of the Corsair logo on the CPU block from default white, to red, green or blue, all from within Windows (if you install this cable). If you don't install the Corsair link cable, the Corsair H80i GT will run at default speeds, which, by the way, is perfectly fine too.

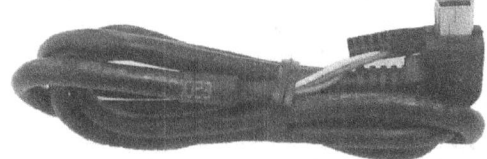

Corsair Link Cable (Shown above)

To install the Corsair link cable, find the cable inside the Corsair H80i GT's box and install one end into the Corsair H80i GT's cooling block.

'Corsair Link' Cable Plugged Into CPU Cooler Block (Shown above)

Attach the other end of the Corsair Link cable into the USB header on the motherboard marked *'USB910'* (only plugs in one way so plug it in the right way round, as below).

Corsair Link Cable Plugged Into a USB Header On The Motherboard (Shown above)

Tie Up Loose Cables

The screw box that arrived inside the computer case will also have some nylon cable ties.

Box For Screws And Nylon Cable Ties (Shown above)
Use these to tie up any loose cables that might get in the way of any fans inside the computer case. You don't want any of the cables stopping the fans from spinning, so tie any loose cables out of the way. This will also make the case look tidier too. Cut the nylon ties where there's an arrow (pictured).

Nylon Cable Tie (As above)

Finishing Off

Have a final check of everything inside the computer case, then screw the side panel back on.

Computer Build Final Check (As above)

At the back of the computer case, plug your monitor into the graphics card.

Graphics Card Ports (As above)

Plug in your keyboard, or your keyboard and mouse combo (wireless or not) into the USB port, as shown below.

Keyboard And Mouse Combo Plugged In (As above)

Plug your speakers in too. Most speakers use one or more of the motherboard's circular sound ports, shown at the bottom of the following picture.

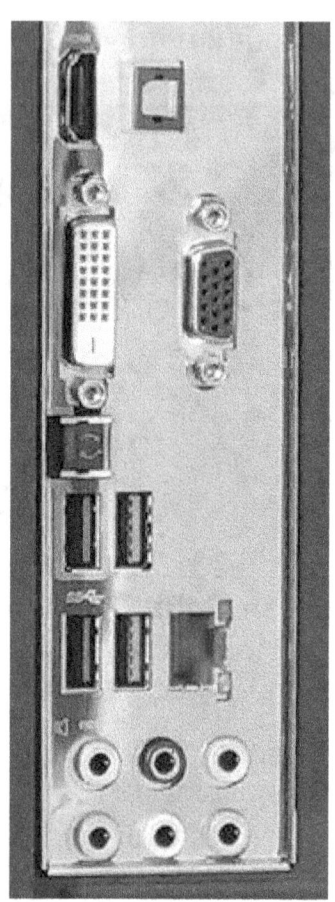

Finally, plug the power cable into the back of the power supply. Plug the other end of the power cable into a wall socket, then turn the power switch on (on the power supply).

Power Cable Plugged Into The Power Supply (As above)

Now turn on your computer using the power button at the front of the computer case.

The BIOS

If you're using the Corsair H80i GT to cool your processor, the first thing you're likely to see on the screen is the message *'CPU Fan Error!'*. If you don't see this message, move on down to *'How To Install Windows 10'*.

This is not a problem. All that's happened is that the CPU fans by default are not spinning fast enough to be detected by the motherboard. So if you do see this message, here's the simple fix. If the screen above is displayed with the message *'CPU Fan Error!'*, press the *'F1'* key on your keyboard. The screen below will then be displayed.

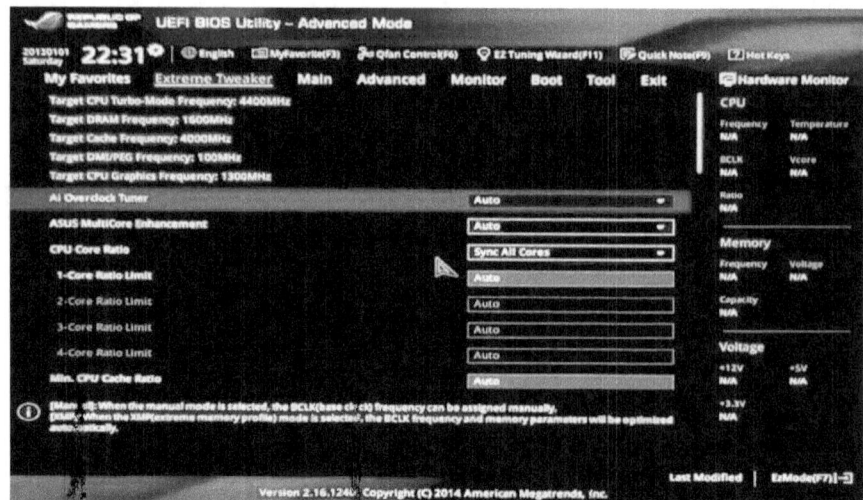

Now press the 'F6' key on your keyboard. This will open the 'Q-Fan Control', as shown below.

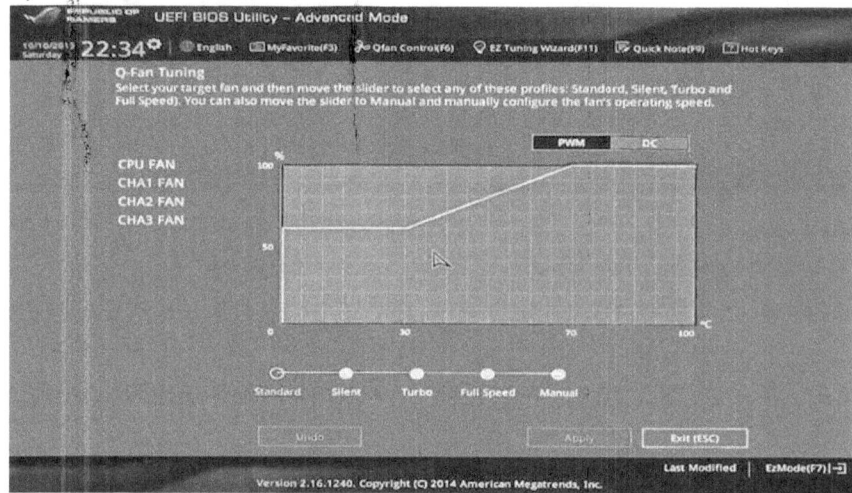

When the screen above is shown, press the right arrow key on your keyboard three times so that the 'Full Speed' option is highlighted, as shown below.

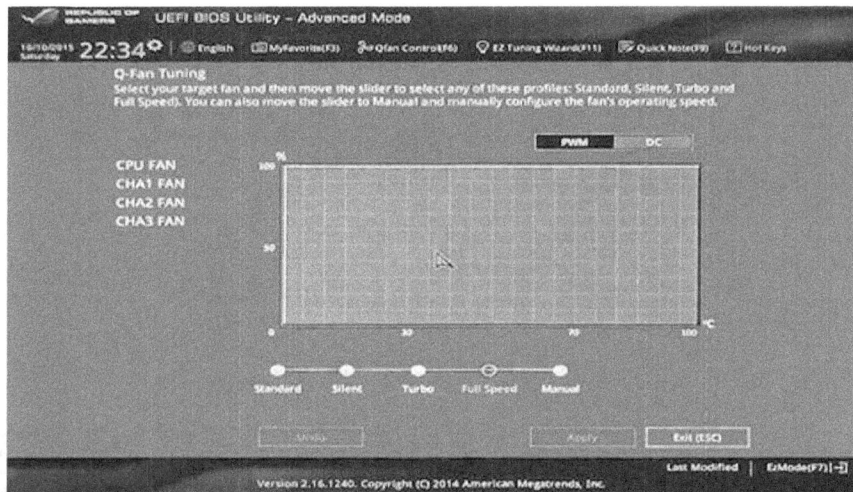

This will turn up the speed of the two fans on the Corsair H80i GT CPU cooler. It won't turn them up to full speed (as you would assume from the above screen), but it will speed up the fans fast enough for them to be detected by the motherboard. They will still be running very quietly.

Next, press the 'Esc' (Escape) key on your keyboard. The screen below will appear.

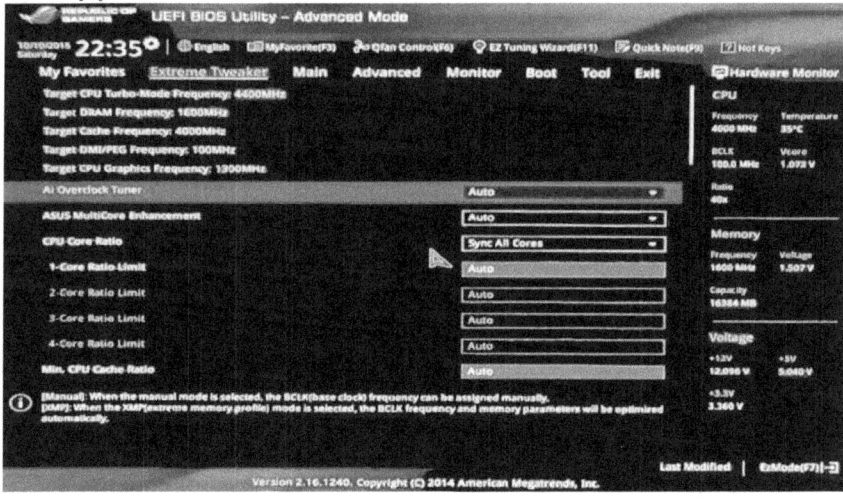

Now press the 'F10' key on your keyboard. The screen below will show.

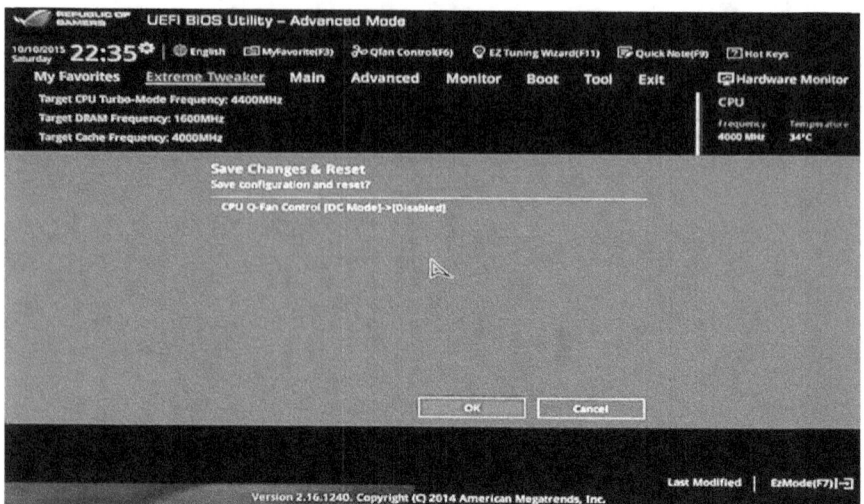

Finally, press the 'Return' key on your keyboard. And that's that problem fixed.

There's nothing else that needs to be changed in the BIOS for this computer. If you didn't receive the message *'CPU Fan Error!'* then there is no need to enter the BIOS at all for this PC.

How To Install Windows 10

So, we're almost there. The computer has been built and now we can install Windows 10.

Firstly, turn your computer off. Next, plug in the Windows 10 USB flash drive at the back of the computer case, as shown below.

Windows 10 USB Flash Drive Plugged In (Shown above)

Now turn your computer on and give it a moment to automatically start up the Windows 10 installation process. If your Windows 10 USB flash drive has a 32 bit and a 64 bit version of Windows 10, the first screen you'll see will ask you which one you want to install. By default, 64 bit will be selected, which is the one we want.

The box shown next will appear on your screen.

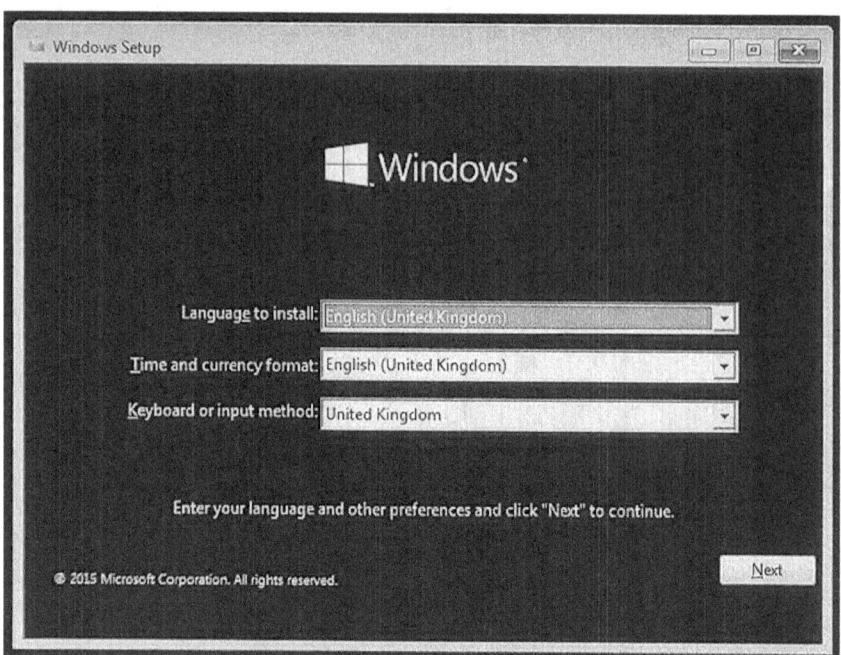

When you see the box above, click on the down arrow to the right of *'Language to install'*, and choose your preferred language. Next, click on the down arrow next to *'Time and currency format'* and choose your preferred setup. Do the same with the third box, then click on *'Next'*.

The next box you'll see is shown below. When you see it, click on *'Install Now'*.

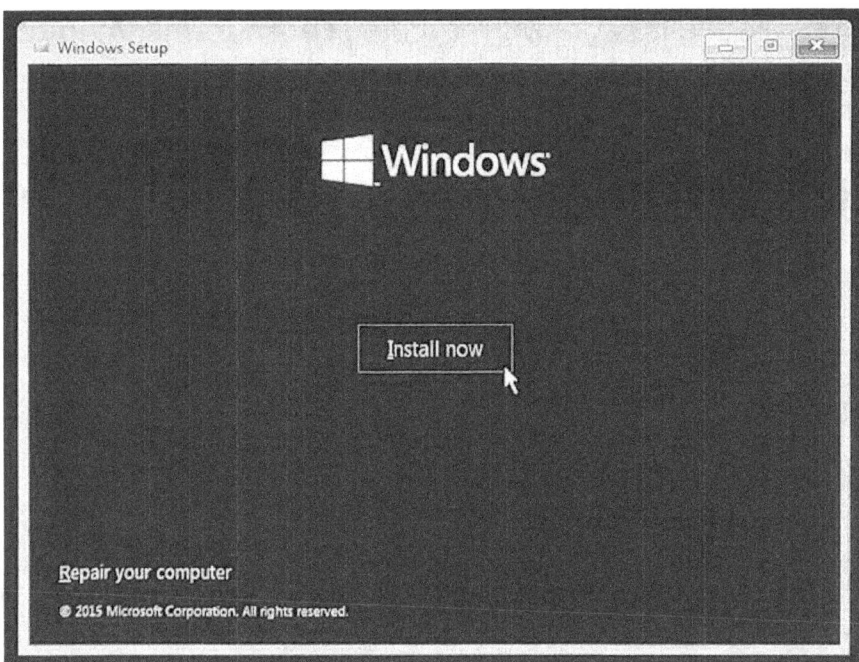

When the box below appears, enter your product key that arrived with Windows 10, then click on *'Next'*.

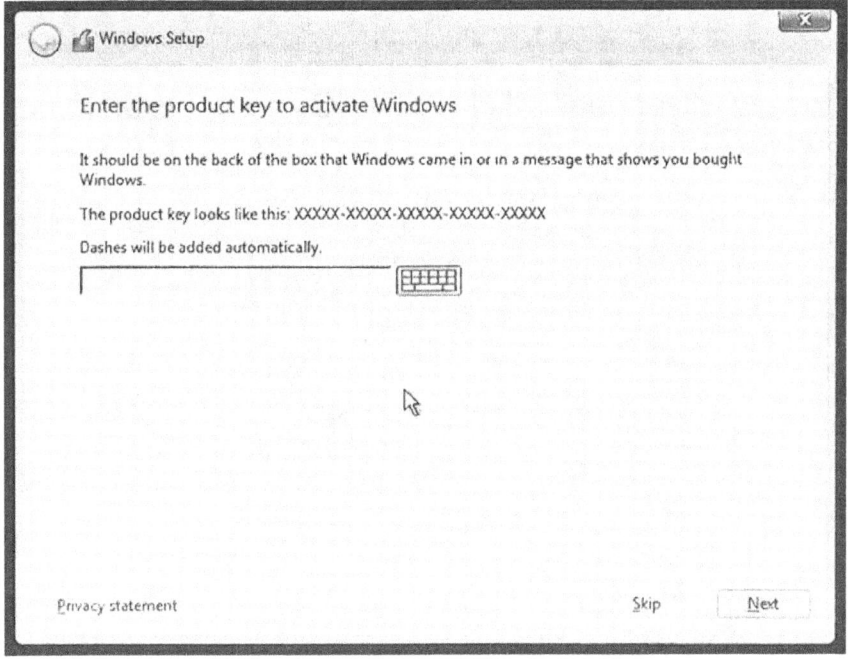

When you see the box below, read the license terms, then click in the box next to *'I accept the licence terms'*. That is of course, if you do accept their terms. Then click on *'Next'*.

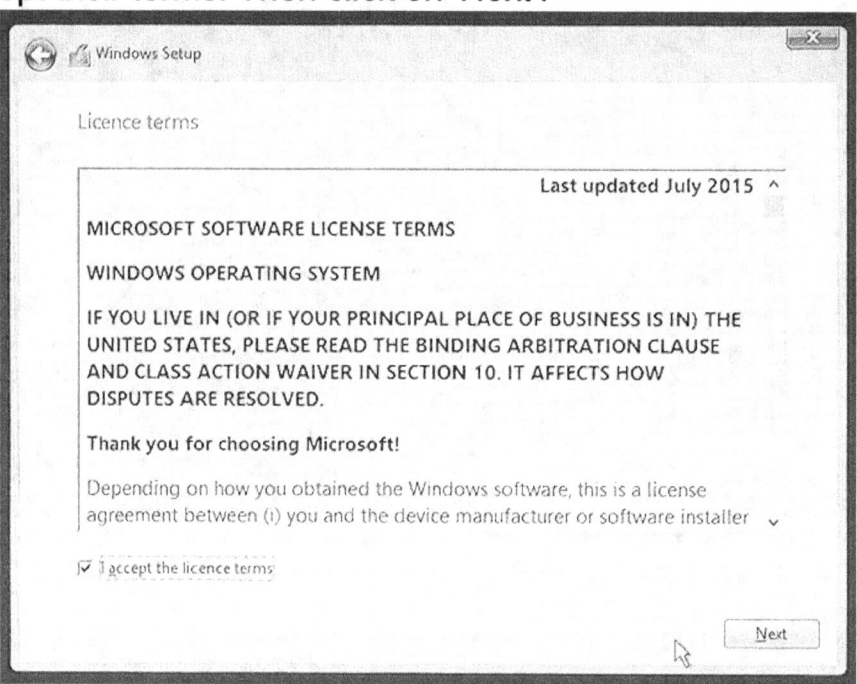

The box below will appear. Click on the *'Custom: Install Windows Only (advanced)'* box.

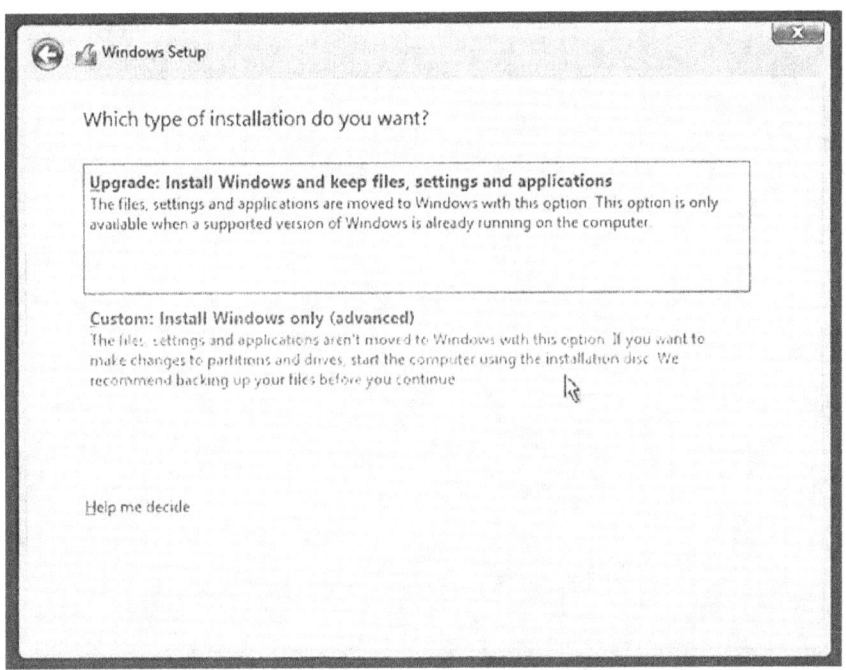

The box below will now show. When it does, you'll want to select the solid state drive (the one that reads *'Total Size – 447.1 GB'*. This is so that Windows will be installed onto the fastest drive we have (the SSD that is). Then click on *'Next'*.

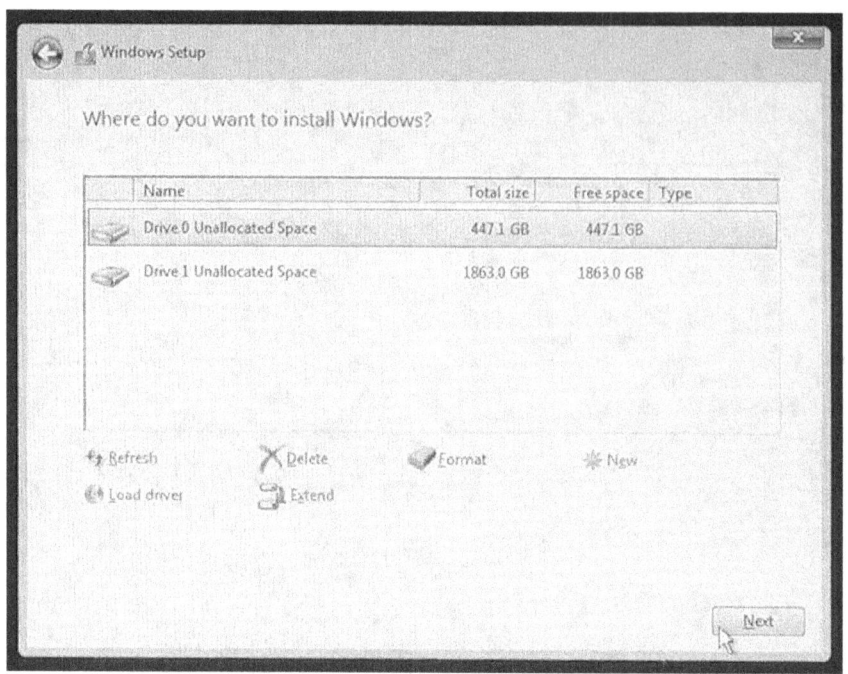

As shown below, Windows 10 will now be installed. Sit back for a moment and let it do its thing. During the process, your computer will restart itself. You don't have to do anything though, it's all done automatically.

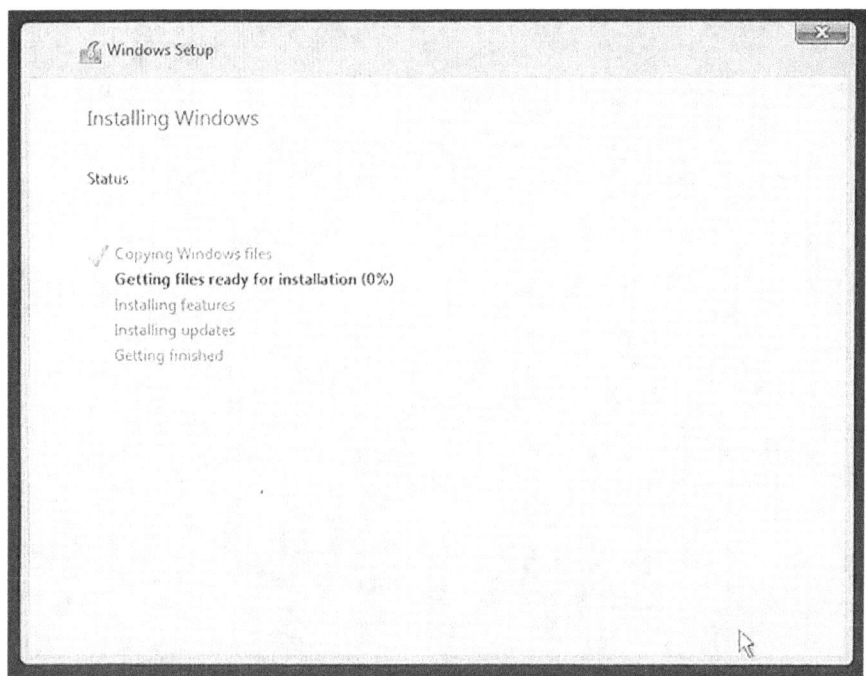

After a short while, the screen below will appear. When it does, click on *'Use Express Settings'* in the bottom right corner of the screen.

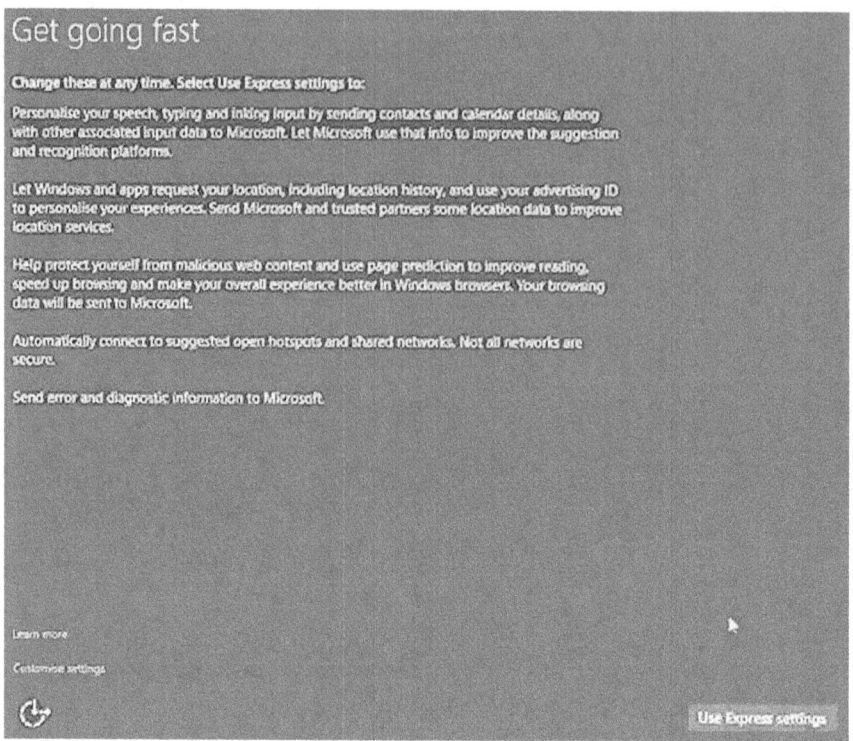

Get going fast

Change these at any time. Select Use Express settings to:

Personalise your speech, typing and inking input by sending contacts and calendar details, along with other associated input data to Microsoft. Let Microsoft use that info to improve the suggestion and recognition platforms.

Let Windows and apps request your location, including location history, and use your advertising ID to personalise your experiences. Send Microsoft and trusted partners some location data to improve location services.

Help protect yourself from malicious web content and use page prediction to improve reading, speed up browsing and make your overall experience better in Windows browsers. Your browsing data will be sent to Microsoft.

Automatically connect to suggested open hotspots and shared networks. Not all networks are secure.

Send error and diagnostic information to Microsoft.

Learn more

Customise settings

Use Express settings

On the screen below, enter a user name in the top line. You can use your first name for this. In the next box, enter a password if you want your computer to be password protected. If you don't want your computer to be password protected, just leave it blank. In the third box, re-enter your password (if you're going to use one). In the fourth box, if you're going to use a password, enter a password hint. This is in case you forget your password. When you're finished here, click on *'Next'* in the bottom right corner of the screen.

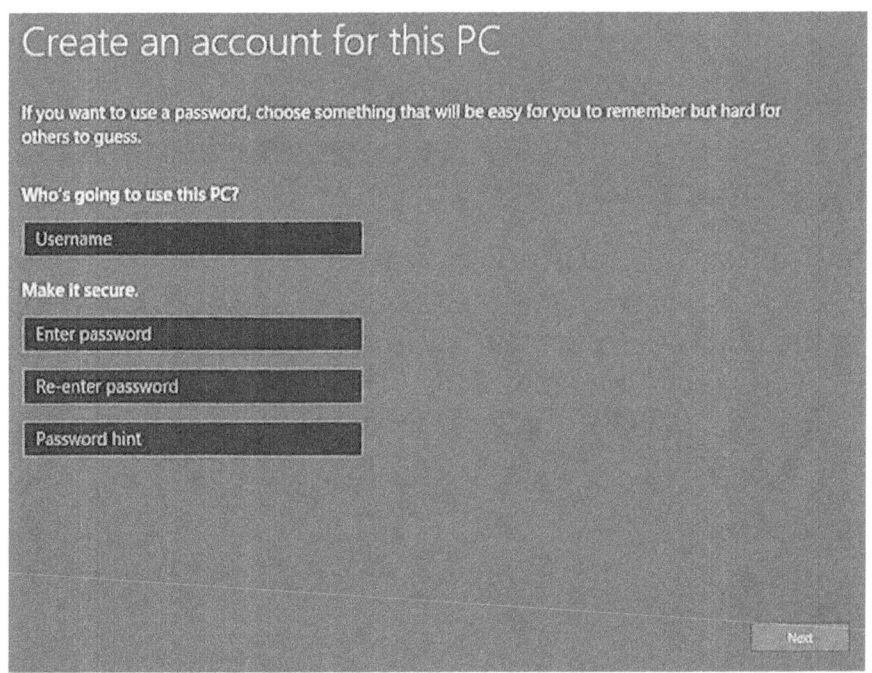

Create an account for this PC

If you want to use a password, choose something that will be easy for you to remember but hard for others to guess.

Who's going to use this PC?

Username

Make it secure.

Enter password

Re-enter password

Password hint

Next

Give your computer a moment and wait for Windows 10 to appear.

Windows 10 Installed (Shown above)

Once you see the Windows 10 desktop on your screen (as above), wait for one minute, then remove the Windows 10 USB flash drive.

Finishing Off

There are a few more things to do before we're done to make this computer completely ready for use.

Making The Hard Disk Drive Appear

Click on the folder icon at the bottom of the screen (as arrowed below at the bottom). In the window that appears, make sure the *'This PC'* icon on the left side of the window has been selected.

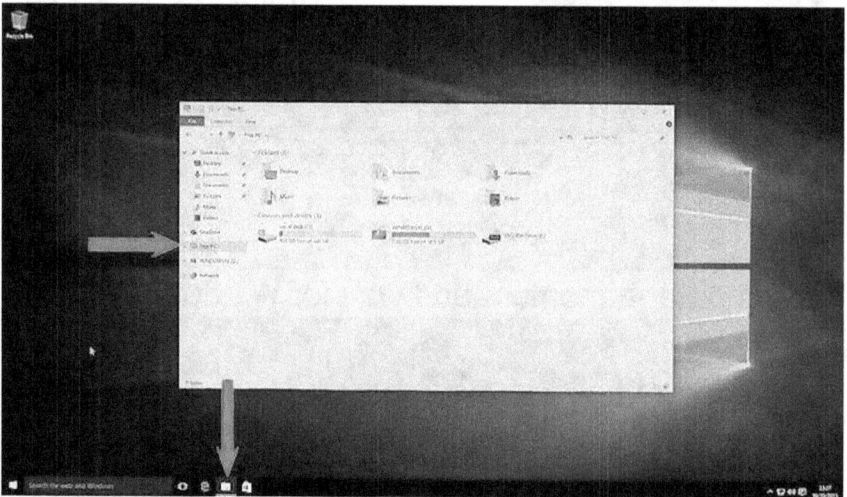

Select The Folder Icon Then Select *'This PC' (Shown above)*

In the middle of the window above, you'll see that the SSD and the DVD drive are there. But there is no HDD appearing. This is because the HDD has not been formatted just yet. So let's do that now so that the HDD is ready for use. This will only take a minute or two.

Click in the search box (as below) and type *'computer management'*, then press the *'Return'* key on your keyboard.

147

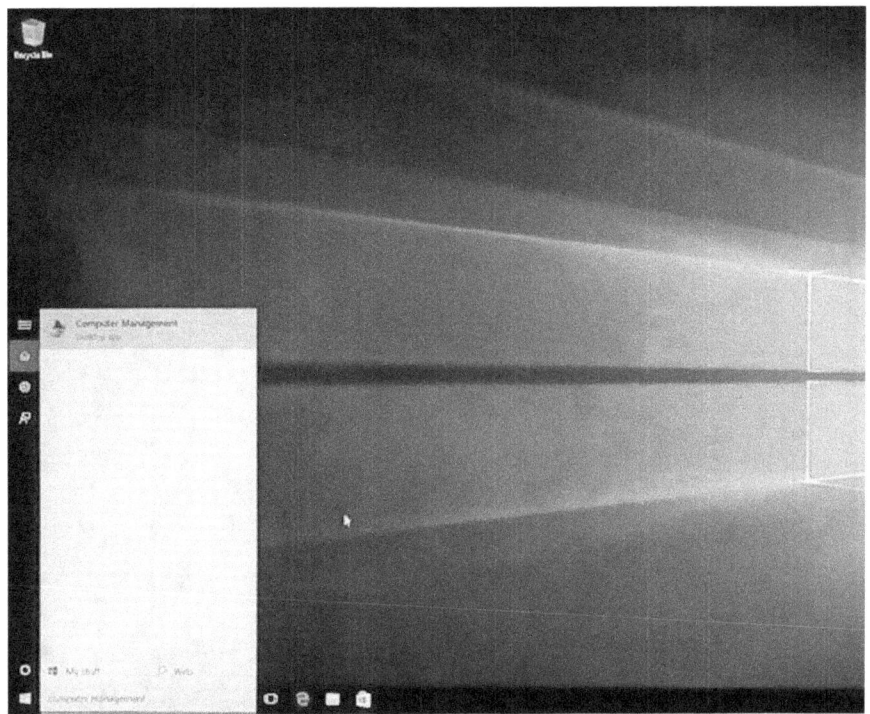

In The Search Box Type *'computer management'*, Then Press
'Return' (Shown above)

The window below will now appear. It's asking you for a partitioning style. 'GPT' is selected by default (which is the best one for our HDD) and that's what we're going to use. So make sure 'GPT' is selected, then click on *'OK'*.

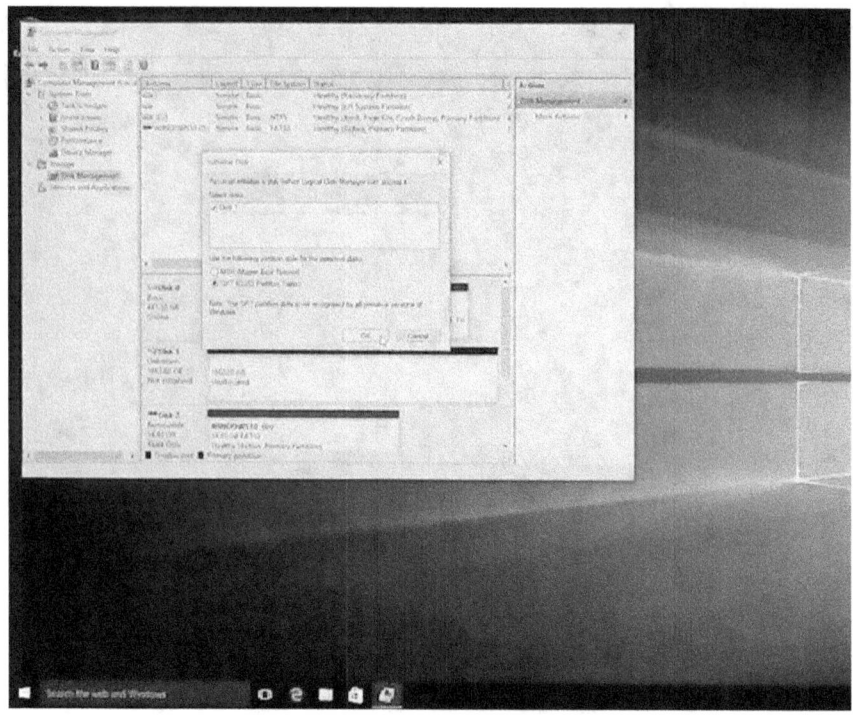

Select *'GPT'* Then Click On *'OK'* (Shown above)

The window below will now show. Right click on the 2TB HDD (the one that reads *'unallocated'*) and select *'New Simple Volume'*.

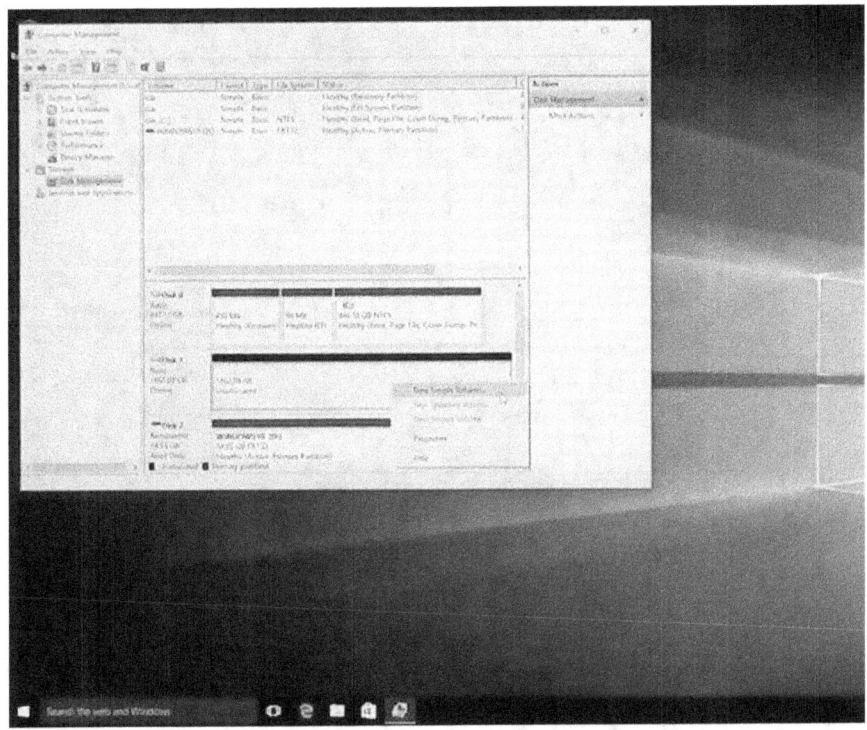

Right Click On The 2TB HDD And Select *'New Simple Volume'*
(Shown above)

The 'New Simple Volume Wizard' will now open (as below), when it does, click on *'Next'*.

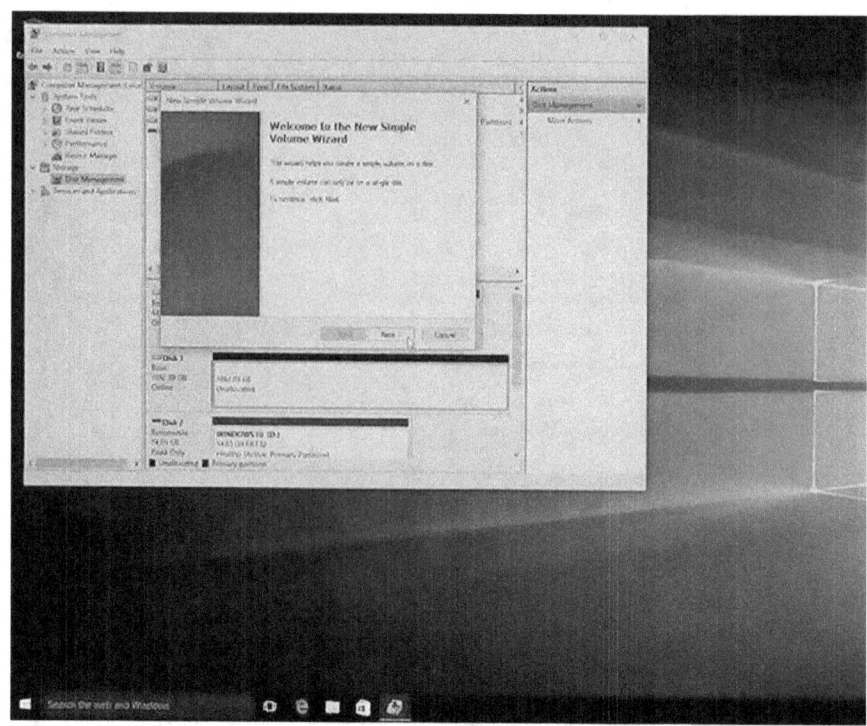

Click On *'Next' (Shown above)*

The screen below will ask what size you would like the partition to be. This can be left as it is so just click on *'Next'*.

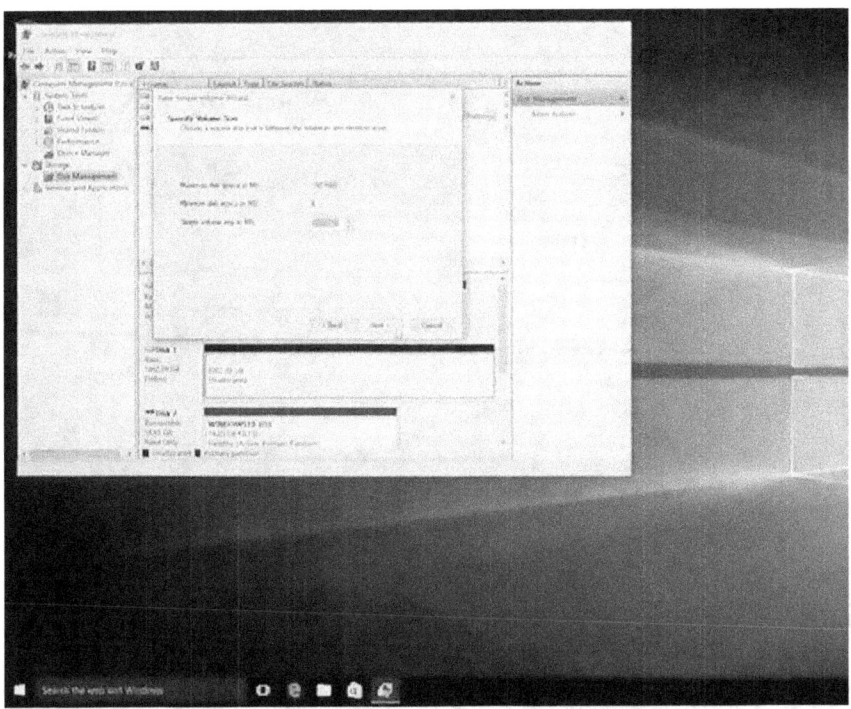

Click On *'Next' (Shown above)*

The screen below is asking if you would like to assign the following drive letter to the HDD. This can also be left as it is so just click on *'Next'*.

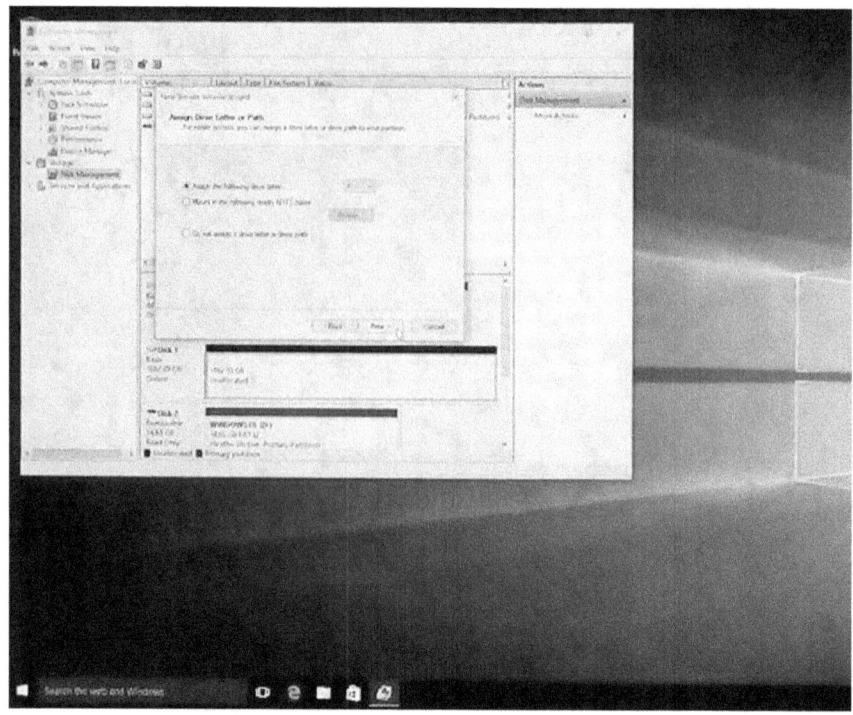

Click On *'Next' (Shown above)*

The screen below will ask how you would like to format the HDD.
This can be left as it is so click on *'Next'*.

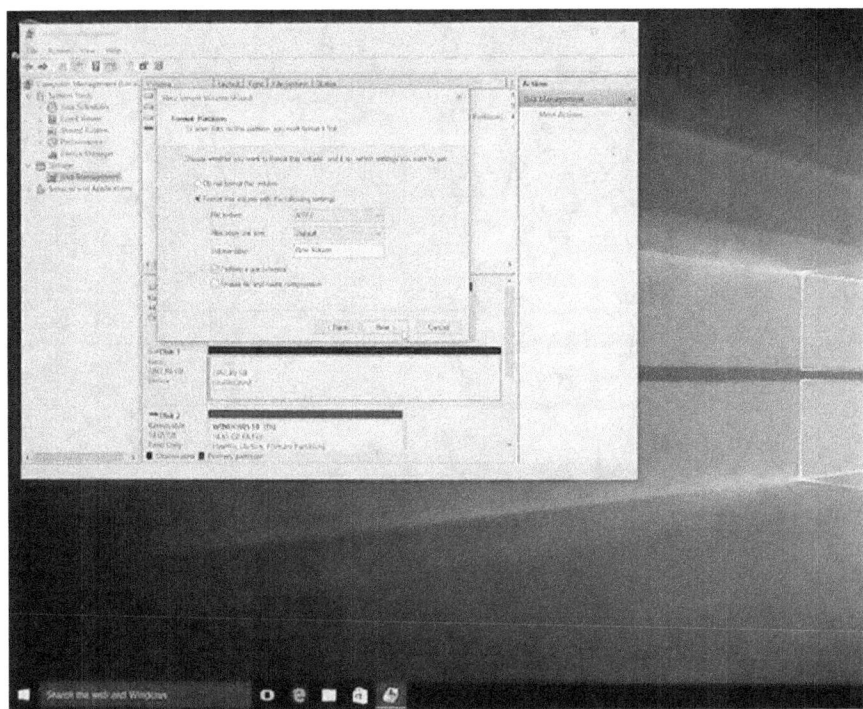

Click On *'Next' (Shown above)*

You will then be shown what's about to happen to the HDD. All you have to do is click on 'Finish'

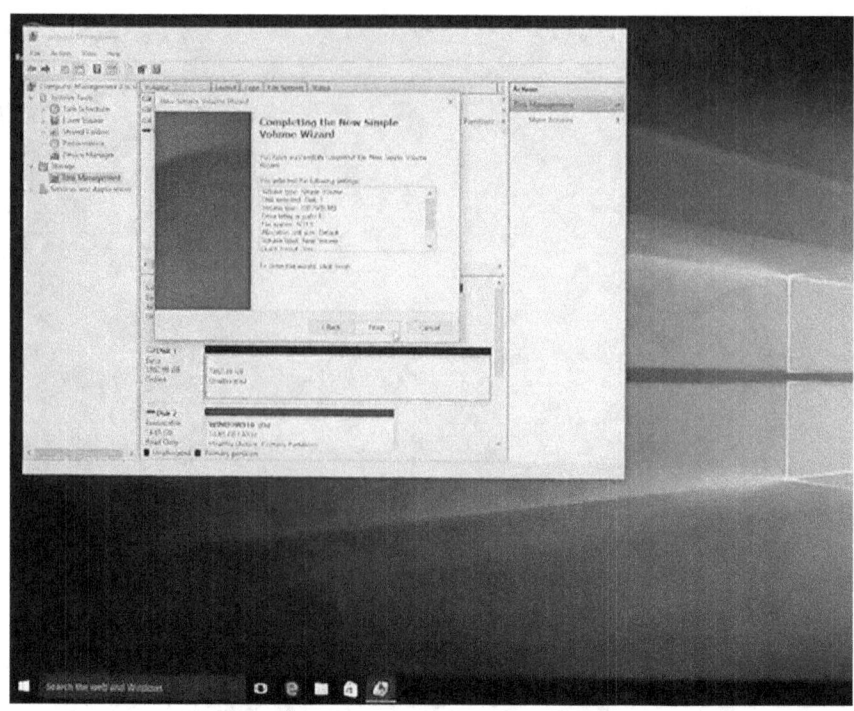

Click On 'Finish' (Shown above)
After a short moment, the HDD will be completely ready for use.

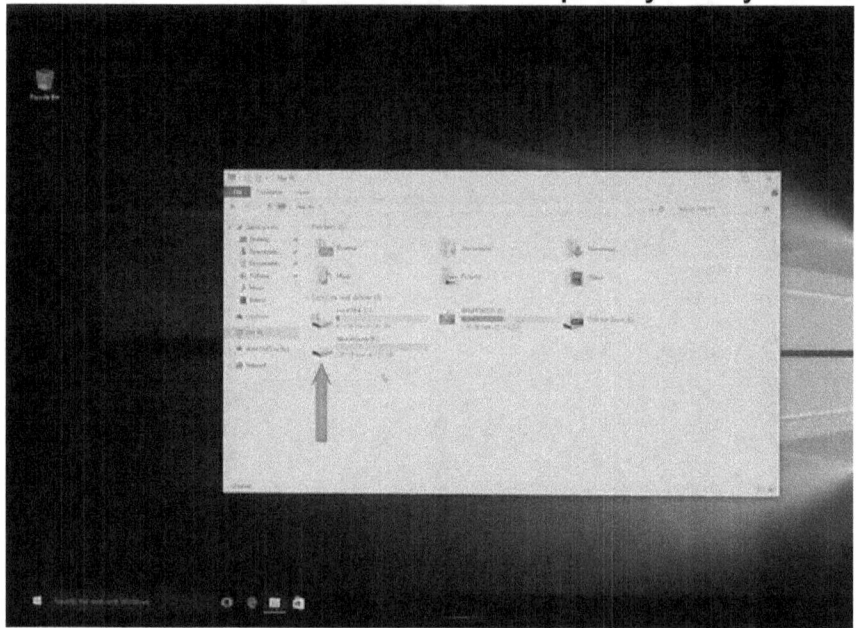

HDD Ready For Use (Shown above)

Installing Drivers

The motherboard's box will have a disk inside it.

Motherboard Disk (Shown above)

Pop the motherboard's disk into the DVD drive. You should see the Windows 10 drivers on the disk. If you don't, you can download the drivers for this particular motherboard from the Asus website at *www.asus.com*. Either way, install the Windows 10 64 bit drivers for your motherboard. This will enable certain things to work such as the LAN port (cabled Internet access) and audio.

Once you're finished installing the motherboard drivers, take the disk that came boxed with the graphics card, pop it into the DVD drive and install the graphics card driver for Windows 10 64 bit. Alternatively, you can download a more up to date graphics card driver from the GeForce website at *www.geforce.com*.

Graphics Card Disk (Shown above)

Once you've installed the graphics card driver, you're computer is ready to use.

Congratulations!!! You've just made your very own computer. Have fun gaming!

www.ingramcontent.com/pod-product-compliance
Lightning Source LLC
Chambersburg PA
CBHW082211290526
45794CB00009B/3503